Irish Castles

Irish Castles

Terence Reeves-Smyth

First published in 1995 by

The Appletree Press Ltd
The Old Potato Station
14 Howard Street South
Belfast BT7 1AP

Tel: +44 (028) 90 24 30 74
Fax: +44 (028) 90 24 67 56
Email: reception@appletree.ie
Web: www.appletree.ie

Irish Castles

ISBN-13: 978 0 86281 991 0
ISBN-10: 0 86281 991 1

Desk and Marketing Editor: Jean Brown
Editor: Jim Black
Designer: Stuart Wilkinson
Production Manager: Paul McAvoy

9 8 7 6 5 4 3 2 1

AP3318

Contents

Contents

Introduction

Ireland is a land of castles. Many hundreds are dotted throughout the country and these, large and small remain a striking and very visible manifestation of the social and military demands of Ireland's medieval landed classes. The earliest fortified residences – as castles may be defined, were built by the Anglo-Normans to consolidate their hold on conquered territories; many were large constructions, reflecting the enormous wealth and power that some of the barons had acquired. However, with the collapse of central authority in the fourteenth century and the resurgence of Gaelic chiefs, the size of castles diminished, while their numbers increased dramatically as every landed gentleman now needed a stronghouse for his own security. Consequently, one of the most ubiquitous monuments of the Irish countryside are the tower houses that the minor gentry built for themselves from 1400 until 1640. The wide use of artillery during the 1641 Rebellion made castles redundant, though this did not prevent Parliamentary troops from systematically slighting huge numbers of castles in the 1650s. Indeed, it seems that most Irish castles may be counted among – to use Marie Lloyd's phrase – "the ruins that Cromwell knocked about a bit".

This book is designed to provide information on a selection of Irish castles that are accessible to the public. Every effort has been made to provide a representative selection, though inevitably the choice reflects both personal taste and the constraints of the book. Many of those included are in good condition and well presented to the public, but visitors are warned that there are others in a dangerous condition, which should be explored with care and which are unsuitable for children. It should not be assumed that castles in state care

are safe, though most are less dangerous and more accessible than those in private ownership.

The castles in this book are arranged alphabetically on an all-Ireland county basis. Practical details are given at the end of each entry, as well as the National Grid Reference (NGR). Further information about castles worth visiting may be obtained in the book *Castles and Stronghouses of Ireland* by Mike Salter (Folly Publications, 1993). The best general account of the subject is Harold Leask's *Irish Castles and Castellated Houses,* published in 1941 but still available in reprint.

Irish Castles

County Antrim

Carrickfergus Castle

The mighty stronghold of Carrickfergus, once the centre of Anglo-Norman power in Ulster, is a remarkably complete and well-preserved early medieval castle that has survived intact despite 750 years of continuous military occupation. From its strategic position on a rocky promontory, originally almost surrounded by sea, the castle commanded Belfast Lough and the land approaches into the walled town that developed beneath its shadow.

The core of the castle was built in the late 1180s by John de Courcy, who conquered east Ulster in 1177 and ruled as a petty king until 1204, when he was ousted by another Norman adventurer, Hugh de Lacy. Initially de Courcy built the inner ward, a small bailey at the end of the promontory with a high polygonal wall and east gate. It had a number of buildings, including a great hall, and must have been very cramped, especially after the keep was built in the north corner.

Probably built in the late 1180s, the keep is a massive four-storey tower, 90 feet high, with a second-storey entrance. Its entry chamber, originally one large, poorly lit room with a double latrine and no fireplace, served as a public room. A shaft gave access to a well below and a mural stair led down to the vaulted storage cellar. De Courcy's curia probably used the third storey; the fourth storey, a high, brightly lit room with windows in all four walls, a fireplace and a single latrine, was the principal chamber and must have served as de Courcy's private quarters.

Following its capture by King John in 1210, the castle passed to the Crown, and constables were appointed to command the place. In 1217 De Serlande was assigned £100 to build a new curtain wall so that the approach along the rock could be protected, as well as the eastern approaches over the sand exposed at low tide.

It was almost certainly Hugh de Lacy who enclosed the remainder of the promontory to form an outer ward, doubling the area of the castle. The ribbed vault over the entrance passage, the murder hole and the massive portcullis at either end of the gatehouse are later insertions, probably part of the remodelling that followed Edward Bruce's long and bitter siege of 1315–16.

After the collapse of the Earldom of Ulster in 1333, the castle remained the Crown's principal residential and administrative centre in the North. During the 16th and 17th centuries a number of improvements were made to accommodate artillery, though these improvements did not prevent the castle from being attacked and captured on many occasions during this time. When General Schomberg besieged and took the castle in 1690, its importance was already in decline. In 1760 it was captured and held by French invaders under the command of Thurot. Later it served as a prison and during the Napoleonic Wars was heavily defended; six guns on the east battery remain of the twenty-two that were used in 1811. For a century it remained a magazine and armoury before being transferred to the Government in 1928 for preservation as an ancient monument.

Carrickfergus. NGR: J 415873.

Dunluce Castle

Like something out of a Tolkien fantasy, the ruins of Dunluce Castle have a desolate, awe-inspiring grandeur as they rise dramatically from a precipitous basaltic rock standing over a hundred feet sheer above the wild and chill northern sea. Separated from the mainland by a deep chasm crossed only by a narrow bridge and penetrated below by a long cave, this precarious rocky outcrop occupied a position of great strategic importance that was fought over for centuries, eventually becoming, in the 16th century, the principal stronghold of the MacDonnells, "Lords of the Isles" and rulers of far-flung territories along the western Scottish seaboard.

Dunluce was probably used as a fort during Early Christian times and a souterrain from this period survives beneath the present ruins. Although the site is mentioned as part of the de

Burgo manor of Dunseverick in the early 14th century, the earliest features of the castle are two large drum towers on the eastern side, both relics of a stronghold built here by the McQuillans after they became lords of the district (known as "the Route") in the late 14th century.

Most of the castle ruins standing today were built by Sorley Boy MacDonnell (1505–89) and his descendants, the first and second Earls of Antrim. The castle had been seized by Sorley Boy in 1558 – although twice evicted, first in 1565 by Shane O'Neill and again in 1584 by the Lord Deputy, Sir John Perrott, Sorley Boy managed, with the aid of artillery, to resume occupation after a short period.

New work carried out at this time included the turretted gatehouse and cannon ports evidently made to accommodate

Dunluce Castle

cannons taken from the nearby wreck of the Spanish Armada ship the Girona in 1588. The north-facing Italianate loggia probably dates to the 1560s; it is a most unusual feature but can be paralleled at a number of Scottish castles. This loggia was blocked by a three-storey gabled house with bay windows and a great hall 28 by 10 metres. It was built in 1636 for Lady Catherine, wife of the second earl of Antrim, and from an inventory is known to have been furnished magnificently. Lady Catherine was believed to have replaced the lower yard after some of its domestic ranges, including the kitchens, fell into the sea carrying with them most of the servants in 1639.

After the Royalist second Earl was arrested at Dunluce in 1642 the family ceased to reside at Dunluce Castle, which gradually fell into decay, though it remained the property of the Earls of Antrim until 1928 when it was transferred to the State for preservation.

On the Antrim coast 3.2 km (2 miles) W of Bushmills. NGR: G 904414.

County Carlow

Ballymoon Castle

Like so many Irish castles, Ballymoon has no recorded history, but on architectural grounds it must have been built c. 1290–1310 and the most likely builders were the Carew family. The castle – as striking as it is unusual – comprises a courtyard about 80 feet square, delimited by granite walls,

8 feet thick and 20 feet high.

The interior is now bare, but the walls' many embrasures, loops, fireplaces and doors bear witness to the former presence of two-storey ranges, some with cellars that delimited the enclosure. The fine double-fireplace on the north belonged to the great hall, while such features as the cross loops allow us to date the castle. It may not have been in use for very long; indeed, some argue it was never finished.

3 km (2 miles) E of Bagenalstown. NGR: S 738615.

Carlow Castle

This great keep was formerly one of the most impressive Norman castles in Ireland. Only the western wall and two towers now survive, the remainder having been accidentally blown up in 1814 by "a ninny-pated physician of the name of Middleton" who leased the building for use as a lunatic asylum and "applied blasts of gunpowder for enlarging the windows and diminishing the walls, and brought down two-thirds of the pile into a rubbishy tumulus in memory of his surpassing presumption and folly".

The original keep was probably built between 1207 and 1213 by William Marshall. It may be the earliest example of a "four-towered" keep in the British Isles and appears to have been directly inspired by French examples, notably Nemours (Seine-et-Marne). The entrance lies at first-floor level in the north wall and access to all storeys was by way of stone stairways in the thickness of the west wall.

Ownership of the castle passed to the Crown in 1306 and was later granted to the Earls of Norfolk, who held it until 1537. It was captured by James FitzGerald in 1494, again by Silken Thomas in 1535, and changed hands a number of times before being purchased by Donough, Earl of Thomond in 1616. It fell to the Confederates in 1642 but was later returned to Thomond after being liberated by Ireton in 1650. Carlow town. NGR: S 718767.

Huntington Castle

The first view of the attractive grey-rendered castle of Huntington leaves one in no doubt that this is a building of great character and antiquity. Approached from the village of Clonegal down a straight 17th-century lime avenue, its front seems hardly to have a straight line anywhere – the side walls gently leaning to one angle and the sash windows lying askew. Additions, alterations and a mixture of styles accumulated over the centuries add enormously to Huntington's charm, while a treasure trove of varied contents reflects family ownership spanning three and a half centuries.

The old core of Huntington Castle is a tower house built between 1625 and 1630. A remarkable yew walk nearby possibly belongs to the 17th century, though claims that these trees were planted as early as the 15th century cannot be entirely discounted. Other formal garden features include a canal and the impressive avenue of lime trees.

The castle remained largely unaltered until 1860 when Alexander Durdin began additions to the rear of the castle.

He also embarked on a disastrous attempt to enlarge the castle's basement windows, causing subsidence in the walls and the collapse of the drawing-room ceiling, which he replaced with a strapwork plaster design.

Aside from the bathrooms with plumbed water – a great rarity in those days – as well as central heating, electricity was also installed in 1888, power for which was generated from a water turbine on the River Derry. Huntington was one of the first country houses in Ireland to have electricity, and in order to satisfy local interest a light was kept burning on the front lawn so that the curious could come up and inspect it.

With its marvellously atmospheric rooms, Huntington is indeed a house of profound character, filled with the spirits of the past. Among the most memorable rooms are the library, the tapestry room and the conservatory, which houses an old vine – a cutting from a plant at Hampton Court dating around 1900. The cheerful drawing-room contains a collection of porcelain including a large famille verte bowl looted by a soldier from the Imperial Palace in Peking. Clonegal village. NGR: S 913607.

County Clare

Bunratty Castle

The fashion for renovating castles and using them to host "medieval banquets" may be said to have begun at Bunratty, which was restored in the 1950s and filled with Lord Gort's magnificent collection of medieval furniture and tapestries. It is

Bunratty Castle

now one of Ireland's main tourist attractions and justifiably so – for no other castle gives a more lasting impression of later medieval life.

The castle once stood on an island in a tidal creek with a view of the water-traffic entering and leaving the port of Limerick. Not surprisingly for such a strategic site, it has had quite a stirring history with a succession of castles from 1251 onwards. The present building was erected between 1450 and 1467 by the Macnamara or MacConmara family. Although of great size, the castle is essentially a tower house. While there are only three storeys in the main body of the castle – with vaulted cellars below the hall – the towers have many floors and small chambers approached by a profusion of winding mural stairs. Many were bedrooms with connecting latrines, the castle having no less than fifteen privies.

The castle's grandeur greatly impressed Archbishop Rinuccini who came here in 1646 and wrote of its great beauty, its ponds and 3,000 head of deer. But the property suffered during the 17th-century wars and towards the end of the 19th century the roof of the great hall was allowed to collapse. It was acquired by Lord Gort in 1954 and since his death the castle and its contents have been held in trust for the nation.

13 km (8 miles) W of Limerick city on the airport road. NGR: R 452610.

Carrigaholt Castle

Set on the verge of a cliff overlooking the Shannon estuary, this is a tall, well-preserved tower house built around the end

19

of the 15th century.

The castle was occupied by Teige Caech "the short-sighted" MacMahon, in 1588 when seven ships of the Spanish Armada anchored at Carrigaholt. The following year the renegade fourth Earl of Thomond captured it after a four-day siege and, in breach of the surrender terms, hanged all the defenders. Ownership then passed to the Earl's brother, Donal, who was responsible for inserting many of the castle's windows as well as the fireplace on the fifth floor, which bears the date 1603. Donal's grandson, the celebrated third Viscount Clare, raised a regiment of horse known as the "Yellow Dragoons" for James II's armies. After the forfeiture of his extensive 57,000-acre estate by the Williamites, the castle was acquired by the Burton family who held it until the present century.

11km (7 miles) SW of Kilkee. NGR: Q 848512.

Gleninagh Castle

Looking down from a hillside across the wide expanse of Galway Bay, this well-preserved 16th-century tower house stands guard over the northern shoreline of the Burren. It has a distinctive L-shaped plan comprising an oblong tower of four storeys with a projecting turret containing a spiral stair. The third storey is vaulted and the dark basement may have been used as a prison.

The castle was built for the O'Loughlins (O'Lochlainns), who were still resident in the 1840s. It remained occupied until the 1890s.

5 km (3 miles) NW of Ballyvaughan off the coast road to Lisdoonvarna. NGR: M 193103.

Lemaneagh Castle

The magnificent ruins of the great O'Brien stronghold of Lemaneagh stand on the fringe of that limestone wilderness known as the Burren. It is a lonely place, some call it bleak, and perhaps a surprising location for a splendid four-storey, high-gabled, early 17th-century mansion. The early part of the building at the east end is, by contrast, a rather grim five-storey tower.

The castle was first mentioned in 1550 when it was granted to Donough O'Brien who was hanged in 1582. By the 1630s it had been inherited by Conor O'Brien, whose wife was the formidable Maire Rua (Maire ni Mahon), about whom there are many tales. It is said that she hung her disobedient men servants by the necks and her maids by the hair from the castle's corbels and used to accompany her husband on raids upon English settlers. When Conor was mortally wounded in a skirmish with Ludlow's army in 1651, she is said to have refused to open the gates to receive her stricken husband, declaring "We need no dead men here", but having found that he was still alive nursed him until his death a few hours later. Ludlow later stayed in the castle for two nights, but found the November weather so foul that he retreated back to Limerick. It was abandoned around 1705 and quickly became a ruin with its lower windows and doors blocked to prevent access.

5 km (3 miles) E of Kilfenora on the Carran/Ballyvaughan Road. NGR: R 233937.

Newtown Castle

Like a rocket on its launch-pad, this unusual 16th-century tower house takes the form of a cylinder impaled upon a pyramid. The castle was originally built by a sept of the O'Briens and later passed into the hands of the O'Loughlins (O'Lochlainns) – self-styled "Princes of the Burren". It was still inhabited by the family at the end of the 19th century, but later fell into ruin. In the 1990s the castle was restored as an exhibition centre for the adjacent Burren Art College.
2.5 km (1.5 miles) SW of Ballyvaughan. NGR: M 217064.

County Cork

Ballynacarriga Castle

The hall or living-room of Irish tower houses sometimes doubled up as a chapel, though rarely were the occupants so devotional as to embellish the room with religious carvings. The Hurleys of Ballynacarriga appear to have been an exception, for the top-floor window embrasures of their castle have stone carvings mostly of a religious nature. One of the windows has a representation of the Crucifixion with the Instruments of Passion nearby – the carvings are dated 1585. The opposite window has intricate carvings around a chessboard design with the figure of a woman with five roses, thought to be the Blessed Virgin, though some believe it to represent the first owner and her five children.

Despite the date on the window soffit of the top floor, the castle was probably built in the mid 16th century or earlier. There is a good sheela-na-gig above the main door, while the remnants of a round corner tower can be seen outside. During the Confederate War of 1641–52, the Hurleys supported their overlord, Lord Muskerry (MacCarthy More), and in consequence the castle was dismantled by Cromwellian troops and their lands forfeited. It is believed that the ruin continued to serve as a chapel until 1815.

7 km (4.5 miles) SW of Ballineen and 1.6 km (1 mile) S of Manch Bridge. NGR: W 290509.

Blarney Castle

Blarney is celebrated the world over for a stone on the parapet that is said to endow whoever kisses it with the eternal gift of eloquence. The origin of this custom is unknown, though the word "blarney", meaning to placate with soft talk or to deceive without offending, probably derives from the stream of unfulfilled promises of Cormac MacDermot MacCarthy to the Lord President of Munster in the 16th century. Having seemingly agreed to deliver his castle to the Crown, he continuously delayed doing so with soft words, which came to be known as "Blarney talk".

The massive castle, which looks even larger because of its picturesque situation on the edge of a cliff, was supposedly built in 1446 by Cormac MacCarthy "the

Blarney Castle

Strong". The MacCarthys held onto the castle with a few interruptions until the Williamite wars, when Donagh MacCarthy supported the losing side and had his estates forfeited. It is said that before leaving he cast the family silver into the lake. The property was acquired by Sir John Jefferys, who built a Gothic-style house onto the castle; this was burnt c. 1820, but a semi-circular staircase tower still remains. Nearby the family made a megalithic garden folly and in 1874 they built a Scottish Baronial-style house overlooking the lake in the park.

8 km (5 miles) NW of Cork city. NGR: W 614753.

Carrigaphooca Castle

Perched on a high rock overlooking the Sullane River this tall tower house commands truly panoramic views of the surrounding landscape. Built by Dermot Mor MacCarthy sometime between 1436 and 1451, it is a very simple building with a single room on each of its five levels. The windows are very plain in form, small and narrow, and like other early tower houses, there are no fireplaces or chimneys.

The MacCarthys of Carrigaphooca were constantly engaged in internecine warfare. They sided with the Crown in 1602 and their stronghold was consequently attacked by Donal Cam O'Sullivan Beare. After a difficult siege the huge wooden door of the castle burned down. The garrison was set free and O'Sullivan Beare retrieved a chest of Spanish gold he had presented to the MacCarthys some months earlier in return for their support against the English. The castle was subsequently owned by the MacCarthys of Drishane until forfeited in 1690.

5km (3 miles) W of Macroom. NGR: W 293734.

Charles Fort

Charles Fort is the most outstanding example of a 17th-century star-shaped fortification to survive in Ireland. It lies on the site of a medieval castle and 1601 it was occupied by a Spanish force and subsequently stormed by Mountjoy's troops.

The construction of the present fort began in 1677. It

Charles Fort

had five bastions; the first two faced the harbour and were the main strength of the fort, but the others were overlooked by the high ground, which proved to be the fort's great weakness. In 1690 it was besieged by the Williamite general, the Duke of Marlborough, who succeeded in making a breach in the wall by placing his cannon on the high ground.

From 1694 onwards the fort was largely rebuilt by the Huguenot military engineer Rudolph Corneille, following the original outline; a barracks for over 300 men was added in the 19th century. In 1922 the army handed over the fort to Irish "Irregulars", who burnt it down. In 1973 it was declared a National Monument and was subsequently renovated.

2.5 km (1.5 miles) SE of Kinsale. NGR: W 655494.

Conna Castle

Resembling some sort of medieval skyscraper, this captivating tower house rises about 85 feet from a great limestone bluff overlooking the lovely rich countryside of the Brade Valley. It was built in the 1550s by Sir Thomas Roe FitzGerald, who by right should have succeeded to the title and vast lands of his father, the fourteenth Earl of Desmond. His claim was disallowed, however, in favour of his younger half-brother, Garrett, who was goaded into a rebellion in which he lost everything, including his life, in 1583. Thomas Roe's claim to the earldom passed to his eldest son James, who was known as the "Sugan Earl" because his claim to the title seemed sure to fail – as indeed it did. After joining the revolt in 1599, the "Sugan Earl" was betrayed by a kinsman, captured and taken to the Tower of London, where he died. That year Conna was taken by the Earl of Essex and partly dismantled. It was later granted to Richard Boyle, Earl of Cork, who repaired the property, but in 1645 it was captured by Confederate forces under Lord Castlehaven and the men of the garrison were put to the sword.

The tower's history came to a sad end in 1653 when it was destroyed by a fire in which the three daughters of the steward were burnt to death. Considering its dramatic history, the castle survives in good condition.

6.5 km (4 miles) W of Tallow. NGR: W 931936.

Coppinger's Court

The striking silhouette of this ivy-clad ruin dominates Ballyvirine – a fertile and picturesque valley west of Rosscarbery. The stronghouse was built sometime after 1612 by Sir Walter Coppinger, whose vigorous desire to develop and modernise his estates brought him into conflict with traditional rural ways. He is therefore remembered, probably wrongly, as an awful despot who lorded it over the district, hanging anyone who disagreed with him from a gallows on a gable end of the Court. He planned to build a model village nearby, but these and other schemes foundered with the 1641 Rebellion, when the house was ransacked and partially burnt down. So impressive was this house that it was said to have had a window for every day of the year, a chimney for every week and a door for every month. Visitors often like to count them all!

3 km (2 miles) W of Rosscarbery. NGR: W 260358.

Kanturk Castle

The construction of the great semi-fortified Jacobean house at Kanturk (c. 1610) was never brought to completion after suspicious neighbours complained that it was too dangerous and powerful a place to be in the hands of a subject. The builder, Dermot MacOwen Macarthy, Lord of Dunhallow, was ordered to stop work, and in a fit of rage he had the stained glass for the windows smashed and dumped in a nearby river. The castle shell was subsequently known as "MacDonagh's Folly".

19 km (12 miles) W of Mallow. NGR: W 382018.

Mallow Castle

The old Desmond fortress on the Blackwater River at Mallow was granted to Sir Thomas Norreys who built a "goodly strong and sumptuous house, upon the ruins of the old castle, with a bawn to it about 120 foot square" sometime between 1593 and 1599. The style is essentially English and early Jacobean with its high gables, single-stepped battlements and large mullioned windows, but the place was well-adapted for Irish conditions with numerous loopholes for muskets. Mallow Castle held out against the Confederates but was severely damaged after being captured by Lord Castlehaven in 1645 and appears to have been abandoned sometime afterwards.

Mallow. NGR: W 562983.

Castledoe

On a remote rocky promontory by the upper reaches of Sheephaven Bay, stands the grim four-storey tower house of Castledoe – one of the most fought-over and disputed castles in Ireland. It was built in the 1520s by MacSweeney Doe, head of a fiery and quarrelsome tributary sept of the O'Donnells, who were constantly engaged in internecine wars usually over possession of the castle, which was besieged and captured at least twenty times before being abandoned at the close of the 17th century.

The halcyon years at Castledoe came during the chieftancy of Eoghan Og II MacSweeny, the foster-father of Red Hugh O'Donnell, who was famed for his hospitality, patronage of the bards and for harbouring shipwrecked sailors of the Spanish Armada.

In 1596 the castle passed to Mulmurry MacSweeney Doe, an unsavoury tyrant who tried disobedient vassals in the castle's great hall; those of the condemned he wished to honour he brained with his club, while the less fortunate were strung up on meat hooks from the castle's parapets. It is said that in order to prevent the marriage of his daughter to Turlough Oge O'Boyle, the unfortunate man was cast into the dungeon and starved to death.

The castle was in ruins by the 1790s, when it was repaired by General Vaughan Harte, and sold in 1864. It was occupied by tenants until the end of the century, but afterwards allowed to fall into ruin again.

3 km (2 miles) NE of Creeslough on the coast. NGR: C 085318.

County Donegal

Donegal Castle

The site of Donegal Castle at the mouth of the River Eske was chief seat to the great clan O'Donnell; the original tower house is believed to have been built in 1474, but existing detail suggests a mid 16th-century date. In 1566 the castle was visited by Sir Henry Sidney, who described it as "...one of the greatest that I ever saw in Ireland in any Irishman's lands and would appear in good keeping one of the fairest". It was burnt in 1589, partly demolished in 1595 and remodelled after 1623. During the Williamite wars the castle was successfully defended against the Jacobite forces. It subsequently fell into decay during the 18th century.

Donegal town.

Greencastle (Northburgh)

At first glance the shattered remains of this castle resemble the magnificent Edwardian fortress at Caernarfon. Indeed, it may have been designed by the same person, though

Donegal Castle

Greencastle – called Northburgh by the Normans – was not a royal castle but was built by the "Red" Earl of Ulster, Richard de Burgo, in 1305 to help subdue the O'Neills and O'Donnells and control the entry into Lough Foyle.

The castle encompasses a lofty rock platform, whose cliffs afforded good protection on the seaward side. Like Caernarfon, it has an oblong plan with the gatehouse at one end and a large polygonal tower dominating the north-east corner. The three-storey gatehouse, which projects from the side of the rock platform, is the most impressive part of the castle and contained the main apartments.

Once completed, the castle quickly became an important port of supply for the English armies in Scotland. Consequently, in 1316 Edward Bruce lost no time in capturing it after he had invaded Ireland. Two years later it reverted back to the Red Earl and later passed to his grandson, William, who was murdered in 1333 – an event that brought about the end of de Burgo power in Ireland. The murder was an act of revenge for the death of his cousin, Walter Burke, whom William had imprisoned at Northburgh the previous year and left to starve to death. It is said that William's sister, moved by Walter's fate, endeavoured to bring him food but was detected and thrown over the battlements to the rocky shore beneath.

A small garrison was maintained here until the 17th century, when it was completely abandoned to the ivy, jackdaws and turf-scented salty air.

E of Greencastle village on the Inishowen shore of Lough Foyle. NGR: C 653403.

Audley's Castle

County Down

Audley's Castle

From its rocky vantage point overlooking the narrow entrance of Strangford Lough, this tower house is a striking landmark whose natural advantages no doubt played a key role in its siting. It was built in the 15th century by the Audleys, one of the families introduced into Lecale by De Courcy in 1177. Internal features include a murder hole in the stair, fireplaces, window seats, cupboard niches and drain holes for slops, while unusually there is a stone vault roofing on the first floor rather than the ground floor.

In 1765 the Wards purchased the property from the descendants of the Audleys, some of whom continued to reside in Audleystown village. During the 1850s, however, the inhabitants of this settlement were shipped to America by the Wards and the area was incorporated into the landscape park.

Audleystown. NGR: J S78506.

Dundrum Castle

One of Ulster's most evocative medieval ruins, Dundrum Castle was founded by the legendary Norman adventurer John de Courcy following his invasion of Ulster in 1177. The site occupies the summit of a rocky hill commanding fine views over Dundrum Bay and the plains of Lecale, controlling access into east Down from the south. De Courcy's original castle may have had defences of earth and timber.

In 1204 de Courcy was expelled from Ulster by Hugh de Lacy who proceeded to strengthen the castle, probably employing master masons from the Welsh Marches. The castle was captured by King John in 1210 and remained Crown property until de Lacy was allowed to return in 1226.

The Maginnis family held it intermittently from the 14th century until the Parliamentarians dismantled it in 1652. The dwelling was ruined by the time it passed to the second Marquess of Downshire in the early 19th century, though the trees on the hill were probably planted at this time. The castle and grounds were placed in State care in 1954. Dundrum village. NGR: J 404370.

Dundrum Castle

Greencastle

A popular 19th-century travel handbook exclaimed of Greencastle, "You would go into ecstasies if you saw such ruins on the Rhine, and quote 'Childe Harold' by the canto." The fortress is impressive, though its dramatic setting at the mouth of Carlingford Lough adds much to its appeal, with views over a sweeping landscape and towering mountains beyond.

The castle was built by Hugh de Lacy almost certainly during the 1230s and from 1280 to 1326 was a favoured residence of the most powerful man in Ireland, Richard de Burgh, the "Red Earl" of Ulster. His daughters were raised here, including Elizabeth, who married Robert Bruce, King of Scotland, although this did not dissuade Edward Bruce from sacking it in 1316. In 1505 it was granted to the Earls of Kildare, but after their downfall in 1534 quickly deteriorated into a "wretched condition". The place was later destroyed by Parliamentary forces in 1652.

Jordan's Castle

Remodelling of the hall in the 15th and 16th centuries gave it much of its present keep-like appearance. For centuries the green below the castle played host to a great fair every August. It was often called "Ram Fair" as a great ram was customarily enthroned on top of the castle's walls. 6.5 km (4 miles) SW of Kilkeel. NGR: J 247119.

Jordan's Castle

Ardglass was an important seaport in post-medieval times, whose defence depended upon a ring of fortified merchants' houses. The largest of these is 15th-century Jordan's Castle overlooking the harbour. Little is known of its history except that it withstood a lengthy siege during the Tyrone Rebellion, when Simon Jordan defended his castle for three years until relieved by Mountjoy in 1601. It probably remained a dwelling until the 17th century, but was a ruin when purchased by the antiquarian F.J. Bigger in 1911, who restored it and bequeathed it to the State in 1926.
Near Ardglass Harbour. NGR: J 560372.

Kilclief Castle

Kilclief was built sometime between 1412 and 1433 as the summer residence of John Sely, the last Bishop and Abbot of Down. Few tower houses can be dated so precisely, but Bishop Sely gained much notoriety for openly living in "castro de Kylcleth" with a married woman. Although the Primate threatened him with suspension and excommunication, the Bishop obstinately persisted and was expelled from his offices. The castle was later garrisoned by the Crown and more recently was used as a farm granary. There is a blocked fireplace with a re-used 13th-century coffin-lid serving as a lintel.

4 km (2.5 miles) S of Strangford.

NGR: J 597457.

Narrow Water Castle

Situated on a strategically important site where the Newry River narrows, this tower house was built by the Government around 1568 at a cost of £361. In 1570 it was described as having "two chambers and a cellar and a hall

Kilclief Castle

Narrow Water Castle

covered with straw and a stable nigh unto the said castle …
and nine cottages covered with earth within the precinct of
the said castle". The walled bawn was extensively restored
in the 19th century, but the modern entrance probably
perpetuates the site of the original gate.

8 km (5 miles) SE of Newry. NGR: J 128194.

County Dublin

Drimnagh Castle

Founded during the 13th century, Drimnagh Castle remained
continuously occupied until 1953. It is a picturesque and
modest-sized building, and its large flooded moat has
recently been repaired as part of the castle's programme of

Dublin Castle

restoration.

The moat probably dates from the late 13th century, but the castle is quite a hotch-potch of different periods. The gateway tower belongs largely to the 16th century, the stone mullioned windows are 17th century, while the entrance porch and stone staircase were added a century later. The great hall was restored in 1988 with a minstrel's gallery, arched sandstone fireplace and trussed oak roof. The formal garden was created in 1990 featuring plants known in Ireland during the 17th century.

1 km (0.6 miles) W of Crumlin Children's Hospital, Long Mile Road.

Dublin Castle

Fragments are all that remain of the great medieval fortress that once served as a symbol of Royal authority in Ireland and the centre of administration. Its construction began in 1204 when King John directed Meiler FitzHenry to make a castle "with good ditches and strong walls". Meiler chose a site on a ridge at the south-east corner of the city walls that was previously occupied by Henry II's "royal palace roofed with wattles" and possibly by a Hiberno-Norse forerunner. It was completed around 1228 and remained more or less intact until the 17th century when it was extensively rebuilt.

The castle was an outstanding example of a "keepless" castle and has been compared to contemporary French castles such as Le Coudray-Salbart. Its east and south walls rose above the natural fosse provided by the River Poddle (now underground), whose waters also fed an artificial moat on its north and west sides.

The castle had a comparatively uneventful history and only ever had to endure one siege, when Silken Thomas made an unsuccessful and rather disorganised attempt to capture it in 1534. For many centuries it was the official residence of the Lords Deputy and Lords Lieutenant of Ireland, the home of State councils, and sometimes Parliament and the Law Courts.

Off Castle Street, Dublin 2. NGR: O 154339.

Dunsoghly Castle

Considering the enormous number of castles in Ireland, it is perhaps surprising that only Dunsoghly has retained its original medieval trussed roof. This has survived because the castle, built around 1450, was continuously occupied until the 1870s by descendants of the same family, despite being cramped and uncomfortable by post-medieval standards. The topmost chamber of the south-west turret was used as a prison and is only accessible through an opening in the vault above it.

There is a small chapel to the south bearing the year 1573 over the door, the Instruments of the Passion and the initials of John Plunkett and his wife Genet Sarsfield. On the west and south are remains of earthwork defences put up during the warfare of the 1640s.

4 km (2.5 miles) NW of Finglas off the Slane Road. NGR: O 118430.

Swords Castle

Swords Castle was built as the manorial residence of the Archbishops of Dublin around 1200. It was never strong in the military sense, but covers a large walled area of nearly 1.5 acres. The adjoining chapel, built in the 13th century, was probably used as the Archbishop's private oratory. Other buildings, recorded for an inquisition in 1326, have now vanished, including the great hall.

The Archbishop abandoned Swords once a new palace was built at Tallagh in 1324 – a move no doubt encouraged by damage sustained during Bruce's campaign of 1317. By 1583, when briefly occupied by Dutch Protestants, it was

Swords Castle

described as "the quite spoiled old castle". It was used as a garden in the 19th century and sold after the Church of Ireland was disestablished.

Swords. NGR: O 182469.

County Fermanagh

Castle Balfour

When Captain Nicholas Pynnar visited Lisnaskea in 1619 he found "great numbers of men at work" building a 70-foot-square bawn and a "castle of the same length, of which one half is built two storeys high, and is to be three storeys and a half high". No definite trace of the bawn survives, but the gaunt ruins of the castle, built by the Scottish planter Sir James Balfour on the site of an important Maguire stronghold, still dominate the town. Just inside the entrance lies a timber stair giving access to the great hall on the first floor. On the ground floor are barrel-vaulted service rooms including a kitchen with a big fireplace and circular brick-built oven.

The castle was refortified in 1652 by Ludlow, the famous commander-in-chief of Cromwell's Irish armies. It was dismantled during the troubles of 1689 but reoccupied by the Balfours and later passed to the Townleys. The building ceased to be inhabited after a fire in 1803 and was acquired by the Crichtons of Crom in 1821.

Lisnaskea. NGR: H 362337.

Castle Balfour

Crom Demesne

Old Crom Castle

Romantic ensemble of ruins and sham ruins set in exquisite parkland on the shores of Lough Erne. At the core of the complex are the remains of a castle built in 1611 by a Scottish planter, Michael Balfour, which in 1629 comprised a bawn 61 feet square with walls 15 feet high, two flankers and a house of "lime and stone" 22 feet square. In 1644 it was acquired by the Crichtons, ancestors of the Earls of Erne, and later enlarged so that the dwelling occupied the whole area of the bawn. It successfully withstood two ferocious Jacobite sieges in 1689, but later succumbed to an accidental fire in 1764 and was never rebuilt.

Today the remains of the castle comprise two gables and a flanker, with the remainder surviving only as foundations. In the 1830s these ruins were transformed into a picturesque folly with the addition of ruined walls and towers forming a sham bawn. Impressive battlemented terraces were also built around the garden to the south, where the famous pair of 400-year-old yews stand, one male and one female, at the site of the original entrance to the plantation castle garden. Crom Demesne 6.5 km (4 miles) W of Newtownbutler. NGR: H 363238.

Enniskillen Castle

All roads in Fermanagh converge on Enniskillen, which commands a vital strategic crossing of the Erne between the Upper and Lower lakes. The first castle was built here around 1415 by Hugh "the Hospitable" Maguire but was retaken many times by the O'Donnells, the O'Neills and the English, until wrecked by Niall Garbh O'Donnell in 1602. The castle became the focus of a plantation town after 1607, when William Cole proceeded to build "a fair house upon the foundation of the old castle with other convenient houses for store and munition". This withstood a Jacobite siege in 1690 and remained the Cole family residence until a fire in 1710; the ruined castle was refurbished as a barracks during the 1790s and remained in military occupation until 1950.

The bawn had two circular and two rectangular flanker towers, but only the south flanker now survives – the so-

Enniskillen Castle

called Watergate – one of the most photographed buildings in Ulster. It has a three-storey façade with stepped Irish battlements and a pair of round conical-roofed turrets. As tall turrets are a feature of late 16th-century architecture in Scotland, it has been argued that the Maguires built it in the 1580s using Scottish masons. Most authorities, however, believe the Watergate was constructed around 1616–19, though it is difficult to imagine a planter like Cole, who did not even own the castle until 1620, spending much-needed resources on such a refined architectural feature just to make the castle look more impressive from the water.

The castle keep now appropriately houses the regimental museum of the Royal Inniskilling Fusiliers. On the

east side of the complex stands the recently constructed Heritage Centre.
Enniskillen. NGR: H 231442.

Monea Castle

Few castle ruins so readily engage the imagination as the picturesquely sited Monea – undoubtedly the most complete and best-preserved of all the Plantation castles of Ulster. Building commenced in 1616 by the Reverend Malcolm Hamilton. Shortly afterwards it was described by Pynnar as "a strong castle of lime and stone being 54 feet long and 20 feet broad". The bawn, comprising "a wall 9 feet in height and 300 feet in circuit" was added shortly before Hamilton was promoted to become Archbishop of Cashel in 1623.

Monea's history is less dramatic than nearby Tully. During the 1641 rebellion it was attacked by Rory Maguire, who "slew and murthered eight Protestants" here, but evidently failed to capture the castle. In 1688 it was occupied by Gustavus Hamilton, the Governor of Enniskillen, who had incurred enormous financial losses in the Williamite wars. His greatly impoverished wife and children continued to live at Monea, but had to sell the estate in 1704. A few decades later the castle was gutted by fire and was subsequently abandoned.

In the last century "a weird woman named Bell McCabe took her residence in a vault beneath one of the towers" until she was evicted by the proprietor, who feared she "might be found dead on the wretched premises" and that some

51

Monea Castle

inquiries might ensue.

9.5 km (6 miles) NW of Enniskillen and 1.6 km (1 mile) E of St Molaise's Church. NGR: H 165494.

Tully Castle

Ireland is full of roofless ruins, but few have had such a tragically brief history as the beautifully sited Plantation castle of Tully. Built between 1612 and 1615 for Sir John Hume, it was gutted and abandoned in the 1641 rebellion. The castle had been surrendered to Rory Maguire on Christmas Eve 1641 by Lady Hume on condition of safe conduct for the local Protestant settlers who had sought refuge with her. However, the "rebels having stripped the inhabitants, except Lady Hume, of all their clothes, imprisoned them in the vaults and cellars" of the castle. The men were bound hand and foot and "thrown into the courtyard where they lay all night". The next day (Christmas Day) the Maguires massacred all sixteen men and sixty-nine women and children, sparing only the Humes. They then pillaged and burnt the castle, which has remained a ruin to this day.

The Maguires would have had difficulty investing the castle by force as it was well protected. When the Commissioners visited the place in 1622 they found it had "a bawne of stone and lime 99 feet long, 9 feet broad, 10 feet high, with 4 flankers. There is also within the bawne a strong castle 54 feet long, 19 feet broad, 3 storeys high, covered with thatch." Of this, the stronghouse survives to almost full height, while the bawn wall and its rectangular flankers are ruined except for the north-east side.

A ten-year programme of repair followed the acquisition of the castle by the Department of Environment in 1974. Excavation revealed that the bawn was divided up by cobbled paths suggesting the use of this area as a garden. In 1988 formal beds were created within these paths using plants known in Ireland during the 17th century.

On the shore of Lough Erne, 5 km (3 miles) N of Derrygonnelly off the Belleek road.

NGR: H 186599.

County Galway

Ardamullivan Castle

Standing on the brow of a secluded valley and surrounded by trees, this is a well-preserved early 16th-century tower house of the O'Shaughnessys. The castle is first mentioned in 1567 on the death of Sir Roger O'Shaughnessy. He was succeeded by his brother Dermot, "the Swarthy", known as "the Queen's O'Shaughnessy" for his support of the Crown. He became very unpopular in the district and indeed among his own family after he betrayed Dr Creagh, the Roman Catholic Archbishop of Armagh, who had sought refuge in the woods on O'Shaughnessy territory. In 1579 his nephew John, popular heir to the family estates and title, fought with Dermot outside the south gate of the castle and both claimants were killed. In the last century the ruin was renovated.

8 km (5 miles) S of Gort due W of the main Ennis Road.

NGR: R 443950.

Aughnanure Castle

The "ferocious O'Flaherties", masters of the whole territory of west Connaught, built this fine castle in the early 16th century, possibly on the site of a 13th-century Norman fortification. It occupies a position of some strength close to Lough Corrib on what is virtually a rocky island formed by the Drimmeen River, separating into two branches and reuniting at the other side – a circumstance that gave rise to the old phrase "Aughnanure, where the salmon come under the castle".

A natural bridge of rock gives access to the inner bawn and tower house on the west. The well-built six-storey tower with a gracefully battered base imparts a very picturesque appearance and commands a wonderful view over Lough Corrib. Aughnanure is unusual in having a double bawn. Its riverside walls have survived whilst an outer wall has collapsed into an underground tributary river (now dry as its course has been changed). However, its pretensions to style are evident from the carvings on the soffits of the window embrasures depicting elaborate vine leaves and clusters of grapes in low relief.

The castle was the seat of the O'Flaherty chiefs until 1572, when it was captured by Sir Edward Fitton. Its position at the head of the lake allowed the castle to play an important role in the Cromwellian blockade of Galway, but afterwards it was forfeited and granted to the Earl of Clanrickard. Somehow the O'Flahertys remained in residence and in 1719 regained ownership, but later the castle passed to Lord St George on the foreclosure of a mortgage. In the 19th century a member of the Leconfield branch of the O'Flahertys planted yew trees about the castle to perpetuate its Gaelic name – the field of the yews. 3 km (2 miles) SE of Oughterard. NGR: M 1544.

Athenry Castle

The great fortress and walled town of Athenry played a vital role in the Anglo-Norman control of East Connaught. Construction of the castle can be dated to between 1235–41 and was undertaken by Meiler de Bermingham after being granted a charter by William de Burgo, the Anglo-Norman conqueror of much of Connaught. It comprises a particularly well-preserved first-floor hall standing isolated within a walled enclosure, which forms part of the town's mural defences. The bailey has been much restored, and there is a round tower at the south-east corner and fragments of another on the north-east. Excavations in 1989 did not resolve the problematic question of the exact location and nature of the entrance, which presumably lay in the south-west corner.

The town's walls were begun in 1312 and considerable lengths can still be seen. Not long after the completion of their walls one of the bloodiest battles of medieval Ireland was fought outside the town between Phelim O'Connor, King of Connaught, and the Anglo-Normans. The defeat of the Irish was so decisive that the constant struggle with the O'Connors came to an end – a process that seems to have resulted in a decline in the importance and strength of the

Athenry Castle

town. It fell an easy prey to Red Hugh O'Donnell in 1596 and never recovered from the damage he inflicted.
Athenry. NGR: M 512288.

Ballylee

The poet W.B. Yeats was so enchanted with this 16th-century tower house beside the Cloon River that he purchased the property in 1916 and restored it. For twelve years Yeats made "Thoor Ballylee" his summer home which he found so "full of history and romance" that he was inspired to write "The Winding Stair" and "The Tower Poems". He once said: "To leave here is to leave beauty behind", and in a letter to Olivia Shakespeare wrote: "We are in our Tower and I am writing poetry as I always do here, and as always happens, no matter how I begin, it becomes love poetry before I am finished with it", and remarked "as you see I have no news, for nothing happens in this blessed place but a stray beggar or a heron."

The castle originally belonged to one of the Burke septs – it stands four storeys high and its original windows still survive in the upper part, though Yeats and his architect installed larger windows in the lower floors. The ground-floor chamber was described by Yeats as "the pleasantest room I have yet seen, a great wide window opening over the river and a round arched door leading to the thatched hall". He also loved the mural stair, symbolically declaring "This winding, gyring, spring treadmill of a stair is my ancestral stair; That Goldsmith and the Dean, Berkeley and Burke have

Ballylee

travelled there."

Ballylee was abandoned and started to fall into ruin in the early 1930s. For the centenary of the poet's birth in 1965, however, the place was fully restored to appear as it was when he lived there. It now also houses an interpretative centre on his life and works. Lest it be forgotten that this was once the poet's home, there is a tablet on the wall commemorating his sojourn here:

I, the poet William Yeats,
With old mill boards and sea-green slates,
And smithy work from the Gort forge,
Restored this tower for my wife George;
And may these characters remain
When all is ruin once again.

6.5 km (4 miles) NE of Gort on a minor road to the W of the Loughrea Road. NGR: N 481062.

Derryhivenny Castle

The building of true castles came more or less to an end in Ireland with the outbreak of war in 1641 – one of the very last being the tower house and bawn at Derryhivenny. Its date is known from an inscription on one of its bartizan corbels which reads "D:O'M ME:FIERI:FECIT 1643" and states that Donal O'Madden built the castle in 1643.

A late date is supported by the absence of vaults on all four storeys of the tower and by its picturesque diagonally

Derryhivenny Castle

disposed Jacobean chimney-stacks. The upper rooms have two- and three-mullioned windows with good fireplaces, including one fine example with a plain chamfered lintel, curved downwards at each end and covered by a chamfered cornice. Along one side of the enclosure opposite the tower there are fragments of a one-storey gabled building, possibly a stable block.

6 km (3.5 miles) N/NE of Portumna, off a minor road lying E of the Eyrecourt Road. NGR: M 872085.

Fiddaun Castle

Fiddaun is a lofty tower house that is best known for having one of the best-preserved bawns in Ireland. Built during the 16th century for the O'Shaughnessys, it comprises an oblong six-storey tower with vaults over its first and fifth floors. There are square bartizans placed very low down at third-floor level, a peculiarly Irish feature that was brought about by the introduction of firearms, which changed the axis of defence from the vertical to the horizontal.

Most of the O'Shaugnessy estates were forfeited in 1697 when the castle's owner, Sir William O'Shaughnessy, fled to France. Though only fifteen in 1690, he had fought as a captain in the Jacobite cause and later in exile pursued a brilliant military career, becoming a Mareschal de Camp in 1734. The castle was continuously inhabited by O'Shaughnessys until 1727.

8 km (5 miles) SW of Gort off the Tubber road, lying on a low-level plain between two lakes. NGR: R 409949.

Fiddaun Castle

Glinsk Castle

In the decades preceding the 1641 Rebellion, a number of Irish landowners were building houses that tried to combine the need for spacious and luxurious living with an adequate means of positive defence. Inevitably, such houses differed from contemporary English manors in having fewer windows, high basements, musketry loops, bartizans and other defensive features. Nonetheless, many succeeded in projecting the air of a gentleman's residence, and few more successfully than Sir Ulick Burke's handsome strong house at Glinsk, probably begun around 1628.

Glinsk was gutted by fire at an early stage and survives as an exceptionally well-preserved ruin. It has a three-bay rectangular plan of three storeys over a raised basement with an attic floor in its high gabled roof. The exact plan of the interior is unknown as there were only timber divisions, but the fireplaces were in the end walls where the stacks rise with tall, elegant shafts that are undoubtedly the best examples of their kind in Ireland.

6.5 km (4 miles) SE of Ballymoe off a minor road to Creggs village. NGR: M 717681.

Pallas Castle

The remarkably complete and well-preserved tower house was built by the Burkes sometime around 1500. It has four storeys and an attic, the third floor being vaulted and the thick end wall containing a tier of mural chambers and a winding stair. There are attractive mullioned windows in the fourth floor and a number of fine fireplaces on various levels, though the oven on the ground floor is a secondary addition. The roof was still thatched in the early part of the present century, the bottom being covered with stone flags for protection.

The tower stands in one corner of a large well-preserved bawn, which has internal steps and parapets, a two-storey gatehouse (rebuilt) and a pair of round flankers with gun ports. Near the tower at the west end, there is a rectangular flanker, an 18th-century malt-house and the remains of a large 17th-century gabled house.

3.2 km (2 miles) E/SE of Duniry off the Portumna Road. NGR: M 757074.

Portumna Castle

It is no exaggeration to describe Portumna as the most important residence to be built in Ireland until Castletown a century later. In grandeur and scale it was without equal when constructed in 1616–18 and like Castletown introduced a new sophistication to Irish architecture. The builder – not surprisingly a man of great wealth and power who moved in court circles – was Richard Burke, fourth Earl of Clanrickarde, Lord President of Connaught and descendant of a Gaelic chieftaincy of Norman origin that ruled much of Connaught for centuries. His house survived the wars of the 17th century, only to be gutted by fire in 1826. In recent years its great shell has been re-roofed by the State.

The building belongs to a distinctive group of spacious semi-fortified rectangular houses with flanking towers at each corner. It rises to a height of three storeys, plus attics, above a raised basement and has an attractive symmetrical fenestration of regularly placed two- and three-mullioned windows and a skyline of battlements of small curved gables with pedestals and balls. At first glance it may not appear fortified, but it was surrounded by a bawn, whose wall and flankers still survive on the north side.

Portumna Castle

From mid 18th-century plans, we know that the interior was laid out in sets of state apartments in the French taste. From accounts of visitors in 1808 it is apparent that the state rooms were fabulously decorated with rich stucco ceilings and friezes, handsome panelling and magnificent furnishings.

The great house was requisitioned in 1634 by the unpopular Lord Deputy Stafford to hold the celebrated inquisitions into the titles of lands in Connaught. It was lost to Henry Cromwell from 1652 to 1660 and again forfeited by William III, but restored to the tenth Earl by Queen Anne. The family continued here in great pomp until the 1826 fire. The castle laid out a fine approach from the north, with its Gothic gates leading into the two great courts in front of the house. The inner court now has a restored Jacobean-style garden, though this would originally have had cut grass and statues. Portumna. NGR: M 852040.

County Kerry

Carrigafoyle Castle

Carrigafoyle has had a stormy history and, although wrecked by a series of bloody sieges, remains a remarkable castle. Cleverly located between the high- and low-water marks on the shore of the Shannon estuary, it comprises a large tower built towards the end of the 15th century by the O'Connors. The tower was protected on the landward side by two square bawns; these extended into the water and enclosed a small dock, so that boats could sail right up to the castle – a rather useful if not unique feature.

The tower has five storeys rising to a height of 86 feet and is beautifully constructed of specially selected small stones laid in neat courses.

In 1580 Sir William Pelham besieged the castle, held by the Earl of Desmond, with fifty Irishmen and sixteen Spaniards. Pelham used artillery brought by sea and within two days had battered down the bawn and the landward side of the castle. All the surviving members of the garrison were hung and the Earl of Desmond's plate, stored in the castle, was sent to Queen Elizabeth I. The castle was later recovered by the O'Connors, only to be surrendered again to Sir George Carew in 1600. It is known to have had a garrison of forty men in 1659 to protect the south shore of the Shannon. Despite its wrecked condition the castle was occupied in the last century by a Dr Fitzmaurice and his family.

3 km (2 miles) N of Ballylongford in the channel between the mainland and Carrig Island. Accessible from the road across a raised path of stones liable to be submerged at very high tides. NGR: Q 988474.

Ross Castle

There are few castles anywhere in Ireland that can boast such a dreamlike enchanted setting as this ruined tower house on the shore of Killarney's Lower Lake. Built in the late 15th century, it is fairly typical of its type, with square bartizans on diagonally opposite corners and a thick end wall containing a tier of chambers and a winding mural stair. The tower stands within a square bawn defended by round corner towers, two of which survive, the others having been removed in 1688 to make room for an extension, the ruins of which remain on the south side of the castle.

The castle was the chief seat of the O'Donaghue Mors, hereditary rulers of this district and descendants of the ancient kings of Munster. After the Desmond rebellion, their fortified lands were acquired by the MacCarthy Mors and later Sir Valentine Browne, ancestor of the Earls of Kenmare. In 1652 the castle was held by Lord Muskerry against a Cromwellian force of 1,500 foot and 700 horse soldiers. It fell after floating batteries were brought over land to bombard it from the lough as well as from the land. The Brownes, who retained the old faith, remained in the castle until they lost their estates in 1690 for supporting the Jacobite cause. Although their lands were recovered around 1720, they were unable to regain possession of the castle, which had been taken over as a military barracks.

2.5 km (1.5 miles) SW of Killarney on Ross Island. NGR: V 949887.

County Kildare

Maynooth Castle

The tides of war have left their mark on the great castle of Maynooth – the chief residence of the all-powerful Earls of

Kildare from the early 14th until the 16th century. Most of the curtain walls have now vanished, but the entrance gate and hall-keep still testify to the castle's former glory.

The massive keep, one of the largest of its kind in Ireland, probably occupies the site of an earlier castle built soon after the conquest by Gerald FitzMaurice, one of Strongbow's associates. Begun sometime around 1210, the building was much altered in 1426 by the sixth Earl of Kildare. What remains now are its eastern walls and towers, together with the main entrance gate on the south – the present entry to the castle.

In one of the first recorded uses of siege guns in Ireland, Sir William Skeffington, Henry VIII's Lord Deputy in Ireland, took Maynooth Castle in 1535 after a week's bombardment. In the "Pardon of Maynooth" – a byword in contemporary Ireland – he put the garrison to the sword despite their having surrendered unconditionally. It was restored to the eleventh Earl of Kildare in 1552, repaired in 1630, taken by the Confederates in 1641 and dismantled at the end of the war. Maynooth. NGR: N 938377.

County Kilkenny

Burnchurch Castle

Many tower houses have an abundance of mural chambers and passages hidden away within their walls, though few have the number and complexity of those found in the early 16th-century castle of the Burncourt FitzGeralds. This well-preserved tower house, occupied until 1817, has four storeys beneath a vault with the principal chamber above, lying just below a gabled roof. Apart from its mullioned windows, this chamber is noteworthy for its finely carved chimney-piece; it has a tall, round chimney, while the roof's gable walls have been extended so that both ends of the tower are carried up an extra stage to provide high battlemented fighting platforms.

A great hall was formerly attached to the tower's outside wall, but this has now vanished, as has most of the bawn. A curved outside staircase still provides access to the three upper floors of this little tower.

6.5 km (4 miles) SW of Kilkenny off the Clonmel Road. NGR: N 472474.

Clara Castle

Anyone with a serious interest in Irish tower houses is sure to be familiar with this well-preserved example, which still retains many of its original oak doors and floor beams. Its survival owes much to having been continuously occupied from the early 16th century, when built by the Shortall family, until the early part of the present century.

The building has four storeys below a vault with a hall, and the entrance leads into a small lobby with a murder hole above. A winding stair occupies the north-east angle of the tower, and a door leads into a dimly lit square room, doubtless used as a store.

On the second floor, in what must have been the lord's

chamber, there is a fine hooded chimney-piece, as well as a mural passage, latrine and a small room to the north, probably a bedroom. More sleeping room was available in the floor above, lying just beneath the vault, where there is also a remarkable secret chamber or strong box only reached through an opening masquerading as a lavatory seat off the top floor chamber. This latter chamber, the largest and best-lit room in the castle, was used for general family living. Its large lintelled fireplace is a secondary insertion, so the fireplace in this room must originally have been in the centre of the floor. The small window beside the fireplace has a sink or slop-stone below, suggesting that dishes were washed and perhaps food was cooked up here. The roof above is a modern erection, while the parapets, which are crenellated in the Irish fashion, are pierced by a large number of pistol- or musket-loops.

9.5 km (6 miles) NE of Kilkenny on a minor road 3 km (2 miles) off the main Carlow Road. NGR: N 573579.

Granagh Castle

Founded by the Le Poer family in the late 13th century, the castle stands dramatically on the north bank of the River Suir just above Waterford. After the attainder and execution for treason of Eustace FitzArnold Le Poer, the castle was granted in 1375 to James, second Earl of Ormonde, whose family retained possession until 1650, when it was captured by the Cromwellian regicide, Colonel Axtel, and subsequently dismantled.

The castle comprised a large, square, walled enclosure with cylindrical corner towers. The landward side was later rebuilt by the Butlers of Ormonde, but the old river façade survives complete with its south-west tower, parts of the north-east tower, the connecting curtain wall and latrines. An adjacent walled enclosure has now largely disappeared, save for a riverside drum tower. In the late 14th century the Butlers built a tall tower house in the north corner of the old castle and this was truncated later in the 15th century by a two-storey hall block built against it. The latter has vestiges of beautifully sculpted ornamentation, including an angel holding the Butler arms which decorates the inside arch of the window from which Margaret, the great Countess of Ormonde, hung rebels.

3 km (2 miles) NW of Waterford on the Carrick-on-Suir Road. NGR: S 171145.

Kilkenny Castle

The imposing ancestral castle of the Ormonde Butlers stands in the south-east corner of the medieval city of Kilkenny in a magnificent location over the River Nore. This great Norman castle has undergone many alterations over the centuries. Strongbow built a castle here as early as 1172 but this structure was destroyed by Donald O'Brien, King of Thomond. It was rebuilt between 1204 and 1213 by Strongbow's son-in-law and successor, William Marshall, Earl of Pembroke. The shape of his superb "keepless" castle – built to a trapezoidal plan with massive drum towers – has been largely preserved despite the many subsequent reconstructions. Excavations in the 1990s indicate that Strongbow's fort determined the basic outline of Marshall's fortress.

After the death of Earl Marshall, the castle was assigned to his eldest daughter and passed through her to the Despencers, who did not reside in Ireland. Parliament often

Kilkenny Castle

met in the castle during the 14th century, which in 1307 comprised "a hall, four towers, a chapel, a motte, and divers other houses necessary to the castle". In 1391 it was sold to the Butlers, Earls of Ormonde, who after the Restoration of 1660 carried out a major rebuilding of the old castle after it had been damaged in Cromwell's siege of 1650.

Except for the classical-style gateway, the whole castle was again rebuilt during the 1820s in an uncompromisingly feudal-revival style for the first Marquess of Ormonde. Largely the creation of William Robertson, the building owes more to the spirit of romance than to historical accuracy. Nonetheless, it retains portions of earlier buildings, including the basic plan and shape of the great medieval fortress – a castle that has served as a princely residence for over eight centuries and played a major role in the country's history.

As befitting a potentate of enormous wealth and power, the new castle was erected on an impressive scale. According to tradition, its remodelling came about in 1826 when the Kilkenny architect William Robertson, who had been walking in the castle courtyard with Lady Ormonde, suddenly paused and pointed out that the main wall was out of alignment and consequently unsafe. This observation gave him the commission to rebuild the castle on a massive scale; as the Marquess of Ormonde was one of Ireland's richest landlords, no expense was spared. The building of sham castles was all the rage at the time, so it was hardly surprising that Robertson should have chosen to recreate the romantic appearance of the medieval castle. He duly swept away all of the first Duke's charming buildings, fortunately leaving the second Duke's classical gateway. The castle that emerged was externally a rather grim essay in neo-feudalism and internally distinguished only by its dullness.

Subsequent alterations to the castle from 1859 to 1862 by Benjamin Woodward and Thomas Deane improved the castle, though it was always the magnificent collection of tapestries, portraits, furniture and above all the famous Ormonde gold plate which redeemed the dark rooms of the interior. It was therefore a tragedy when the contents were sold in 1935 when the Ormondes ceased to live in the castle, bringing to an end the centuries-old occupation. In 1967 the sixth Marquess gave the castle to a local preservation society who two years later transferred it to the State to be restored and managed on behalf of the nation.

Extensive restoration began in 1973, but as yet only portions of the castle are open to the public. This includes the hall, which retains its fine 18th-century flagged floor and walls that were once covered with gilded Spanish leather, while its elaborate ceiling is a modern replica of the original. The great mahogany staircase brings the visitor to the dining-room, located in the circular north-east tower with its 12-foot-thick walls; a further set of stairs winds upwards to a corridor leading to the principal restored room of the castle – the picture gallery. Occupying the entire length of the castle's east wing, it measures 150 feet long, 27 feet wide and 30 feet high to the apex of the hammer-beamed roof. Between 1859 and 1862 Benjamin Woodward introduced a partly glazed roof so that this immense space could be lit, while John Hungerford Pollen painted the roof trusses in the pre-

Raphaelite style. Pollen was also responsible for the white Carrara marble double chimney-piece which he carved himself, complete with a series of bas-reliefs illustrating important events in the Butler family history. The walls of this room are again lined with pictures, and although these are but a few compared to the 184 paintings it once contained, some of the magic and grandeur of this room has now been restored.

Kilkenny city. NGR: S 509557.

County Laois

Dunamase Castle

The battered remains of this once-strong castle crowns a massive rock with superb views over the pass through the west Wicklow hills. It was built in the 13th century by William Marshall and his son-in-law William de Braose on the site of an Irish fort that Strongbow had obtained. It had a number of owners, notably Roger de Mortimer – who further fortified it – before it fell into the hands of the O'Mores in the 14th century. In 1641 it was taken from the O'Mores by Sir Charles Coote, retaken by Eoghan O'Neill in 1646 and finally captured and dismantled by the Cromwellians in 1650.

William Marshall probably began the enormous rectangular tower on top of the hill. Much of the southern part has now vanished, while the northern portion was remodelled to form a stronghouse in the 16th century and a tower was added to the west wall flanking the entrance. The surrounding walls of the inner bailey were probably built by William de Braose around 1250. These are strongest on the vulnerable east side where there is a gateway flanked by oblong towers containing guard rooms.

5 km (3 miles) W of Stradbally off the N80 Portlaoise Road. NGR: S 523980.

Lea (Leghe) Castle

Cromwellian troops dismantled some of Ireland's finest castles – not least of which was the great fortress of Lea. The core of the castle is a massive four-towered keep that bears such a striking resemblance to Carlow Castle that they must be contemporary, especially as both were owned by William Marshall. It therefore belongs to the early 13th century and if so, it must be one of the earliest of these distinctive castles comprising a rectangular block with cylindrical corner towers. Sadly, only one tower now stands to any height, but the main block had three storeys over a basement and like Carlow has a first-floor doorway by the north-east tower and a straight stair in the north wall. Few castles have had such an active history. Lea was burnt in 1285 by the O'Connors, in 1307 by O'More and in 1315 by Bruce, after which the adjacent town was abandoned. The castle was subsequently captured on many occasions and passed to the O'Mores, the FitzGeralds, the Earls of Ormonde and the O'Dempseys, before Cromwellian troops finally wrecked it in 1650. In the 18th century the celebrated horse-thief James Dempsey used the vaults of the keep as his stables.

4 km (2.5 miles) E of Portarlington on a minor road N of the Monasterevin Road. NGR: N 571121.

County Leitrim

Parke's Castle

Rising from the tranquil waters of Lough Gill, this attractive Plantation castle has recently undergone an extensive restoration. It now appears much as it did around 1610 when Robert Parker completed his fortified manor house on the site of a 15th-century O'Rorke castle. The walls of the original bawn were retained, but the O'Rorke tower house in the centre was demolished and its stones used to build the three-storey manor. This has now had its window glazing reinstated, while local craftsmen have successfully restored the timber stair, as well as the mortice and tenon oak roof. One of two round flankers forms one end of the manor, while at the other end stands a gatebuilding with an arched entrance leading into the enclosure. There is also a postern gate and a sally port, though there are no flankers on the lake shore probably as the water level was 10 feet higher in the 17th century and lapped up against the bawn walls. No doubt these waters fed the moat that formerly surrounded the bawn.

Excavations in the 1970s revealed the base of the O'Rorke tower house beneath the courtyard cobbles and this is now exposed to view. It was in this tower that Francisco de Cuellar, the shipwrecked Armada officer, was entertained by

Parke's Castle

Brian O'Rorke. In later years de Cuellar was to write of his host: "Although this chief is a savage, he is a good Christian and an enemy of the heretics and is always at war with them." He was eventually captured, indicted and executed for high treason in London in 1591. The Parkers, who subsequently acquired his confiscated property, remained at Newtown, or Leitrim Castle – as it was formerly known – until the end of the 17th century, when it was deserted.

6.5 km (4 miles) NW of Dromahaire on the Sligo Road beside Lough Gill. NGR: G 783354.

County Limerick

Adare Castle

The time-worn remains of this Anglo-Norman fortress on the banks of the River Maigue may be counted among the most impressive castles in Ireland. It was first mentioned in 1226 as being held by Geoffrey de Marisco, but later passed to the FitzGeralds, possibly as early as 1240. The Earls of Kildare retained ownership for nearly 300 years until Silken Thomas's rebellion of 1536, when it was forfeited and granted to the Earl of Desmond. Barely forty years later, in 1578, the Munster Geraldines were themselves in rebellion and lost the castle to English troops after an eleven-day siege. Attempts to retrieve the castle resulted in a series of notably bloody sieges in 1579, 1581 and 1600, leaving the fabric badly damaged. It was finally dismantled by Parliamentary troops in 1657.

The castle was probably begun in the 1190s and initially comprised a large square tower; this was remodelled in the 15th century and is thus difficult to assess confidently. No doubt it served as the lord's accommodation and thus complemented the more public function of the Great Hall by the river, which was clearly built to entertain visitors.

The curtain walls around the inner ward and along the west side of the outer ward were possibly built around 1240, no doubt replacing timber palisades. The very ruined aisled Great Hall may have been added in 1326 when the second Earl of Kildare undertook extensive works at the castle. It is flanked by kitchens and service rooms, which extend to the eastern perimeter of the outer ward – whose well-preserved battlemented walls may be largely 15th century in date.

14.5 km (9 miles) SW of Limerick city. NGR: R 471467.

Askeaton Castle

The splendid castle of the Munster Geraldines at Askeaton, the principal seat of the last Earls of Desmond, rises majestically above the River Deel on a small rocky island. Most of the ruins belong to the 15th century, though they incorporate parts of a much older fortress that was founded here by William de Burgo in 1199. The Earls of Desmond had many changes in fortune after they acquired the place in the 1340s, but the heyday of their great wealth and power undoubtedly came when the King, otherwise engaged in French wars, surrendered his royal rights in Munster to the seventh Earl of Desmond. It was during this time from 1420 to 1457 that most of the castle and nearby Franciscan friary were built.

The castle extends over two courtyards – an upper ward crowning the rock and a lower ward surrounding it. The upper ward still retains fragments of its 13th-century polygonal wall with footings of a gateway on the east side. At the northern end stands a large 15th-century hall and chamber block, probably on 13th-century foundations. In the outer ward, built against the ramparts on the west side, stands the celebrated banqueting hall – perhaps the finest secular building of its period in Ireland.

Its foundations are early medieval, but the ground floor vaulted chambers, cellars and kitchens all belong to the 1430s, when the seventh Earl built the hall above – a magnificent room 72 feet long and 30 feet wide. A striking feature are the large windows with decorated carvings, while the south end is decorated with a blind arcade, behind which stands the remains of a chapel block.

During the Desmond rebellion in 1580, the castle fell to Pelham after two days' bombardment, and shortly afterwards was handed over to the Berkleys. In 1599 the Earl of Essex came to its relief after it had withstood a 147-day siege by the "Sugan" Earl of Desmond. It was captured by the Confederates in 1642 and ten years later dismantled by Cromwellian troops.

25.5 km (16 miles) W/SW of Limerick city on the T68. NGR: R 341501.

Carrigogunnell Castle

From its superb vantage point on a volcanic crag, this fortress is a striking landmark which demonstrates an excellent use of natural defences. It is mentioned in 13th-century contexts, but the greater part of the present remains belong to the period after 1449 when the sixth Earl of Desmond conferred it on Brien Duff O'Brien, son of the Prince of Thomond. It has a rather complex range of buildings, including a four-storey tower, a circular bastion and a gabled house. In 1536 the castle was surrendered to Lord Deputy Grey, after he used his artillery to blow up the gate of the outer court. The men of the garrison, who were found huddled in the dungeon, were all taken out and executed. The O'Briens later lost the castle in the Cromwellian forfeitures. In 1691 it was mined and blown up with an enormous quantity of gunpowder by order of General Ginkel, after it had surrendered with its Jacobite garrison of 150 men. Located 2 miles NW of Mungret. NGR: R 499552.

Limerick Castle

This striking landmark in Limerick, known as "King John's Castle", stands on the east bank of the Shannon within the city walls, commanding a strategically important river crossing. It was built as a royal fortress in the early 13th century and is an outstanding example of a "keepless" castle, similar in many respects to contemporary castles at Kilkenny and Dublin. It has a pentagonal plan with massive drum towers defending each of the four main angles – one of which was replaced by a diamond-shaped bastion in 1611.

The Normans appear to have attempted to secure control of Limerick around 1202 when the Annals record a "castle there". Stone-revetted earthen banks, recently discovered during excavations, may be part of this early Norman fort. Work on the stone castle may have begun a little later, perhaps around 1210, as the Pipe Rolls record an expenditure of £733 on the site in 1212.

For most of its history the castle remained in Crown control and had an uninterrupted line of constables from 1216 until the death of Lord Gort in 1842. Despite this continuity, the castle did not escape being captured on many occasions. It fell to Bruce in 1316 and later again to the O'Briens and MacNamaras in 1369. In 1642 it was taken by a strong force of Irish, after they ignited mines and breached the walls. Recent excavations in the vicinity of the east curtain wall have uncovered a fascinating series of mines and countermines dug during this siege. The castle was captured by Cromwellian troops in 1651 and by Williamite troops in 1691.

In the 18th century the towers were reduced in height and fitted to bear artillery. Barrack buildings were also completed in 1751 and remained in use until 1922. These were partly replaced by Corporation houses in 1935, but in 1990 the whole interior was cleared and a new visitor centre erected. Ongoing archaeological excavation, supported by Shannon Heritage, continues in the castle every summer. Limerick city. NGR: R 582576.

Shanid Castle

The famous war-cry and motto of the Earls of Desmond "Shanid aboo", echoed a belief that this little castle was "Desmond's first and most ancient house". It was built by Thomas FitzGerald, after he had been granted the land around 1198. The castle comprises the shattered shell of a polygonal tower spectacularly clinging to the summit of a large earthen motte with surrounding fosse and bank. The tower is circular internally and only half survives to full parapet height. It was surrounded by a curtain wall around the summit of the earthwork; the remains on the south side still retain some of their battlements and loop-holes. A small kidney-shaped bailey on the east side has no sign of an enclosing wall. It was captured by Red Hugh O'Donnell in 1601 and wrecked in 1641.

13 km (8 miles) N of Newcastle West. NGR: R 243452.

County Louth

Carlingford Castle

Looking down from a rock above the medieval walled town, this striking fortress stands guard over the harbour and the narrow pass between the town and the lofty mountains of the Cooley Peninsula. Historical references to the castle are sparse, but on architectural grounds it was most likely begun around 1200, probably by Hugh de Lacy. King John stayed here for three days in 1210, and later that century the

Carlingford Castle

eastern side of the castle was remodelled.

The original fortification evidently consisted of a many-sided curtain wall enclosing a roughly oval area around the summit of the rock. This survives around the western portion of the castle's courtyard, together with a flanking tower and the remains of a twin-towered gatehouse. Only portions of the northern gatehouse tower survive, but it is evident the gate towers flanked a surprisingly narrow entrance passage. The well-preserved square tower is noteworthy for the way its plan changes to a half-octagon on the upper levels.

The massive cross-wall of the castle was probably added in 1262 when records in a pipe roll show substantial payments being made for stone, timber and lead for building works at Carlingford. At this time, much of the eastern section of the castle was also remodelled to create three-storey apartments and a great hall. A four-storey range was added in the 15th century; this is now ruined but has some interesting fireplaces and arcading.

Carlingford appears to have remained in English hands during the post-medieval period. In 1596 Hugh O'Neill, Earl of Tyrone, tried to take the castle in a surprise attack. It was captured by Sir Henry Tichborne (Royalist) in 1642, surrendered to Lord Inchiquin (Royalist) in 1649 and delivered up to Sir Charles Coote (Cromwellian) the following year. It is likely Coote dismantled the castle, for it plays no further role in Irish history, though the town was used as a hospital station during the Williamite wars.
Carlingford town. NGR: J 188120.

Castleroche

Still known by its simple Norman-French name of Roche, this impressive castle clings dramatically to the summit of a great rocky outcrop. Striking and powerful, it commands a pass northwards and affords wonderful views over the surrounding country. According to the Close Rolls of 1236, it was raised by Lady Rohesia de Vernon, whose grandfather came to Ireland with Prince John in 1185. There is a tale that she promised herself in marriage to the architect if he completed the job to her satisfaction, but when he came to claim her hand, she had him cast from one of the windows in the west end – still popularly known as the "Murder Window".

Most of the castle was built in the 1230s, though it may have been completed in the following decade. Its peculiar triangular layout, determined by the shape of the rock, comprises a large enceinte enclosure with a twin-towered gatehouse linked to the very considerable Great Hall. A causeway gives access to the entrance across a rock-cut ditch, in the centre of which was a gap with drawbridge protected by a barbican.

The large rectangular hall must have been an impressive building in its heyday. Its main chamber, lit on the south side by three large windows, was so enormous that the basement must have had timber subdividing to support the floor. The east gabled wall survives with some traces of the old roof line and indications of a third storey. A small rectangular building on the north side of the hall is a later addition, while the remains of a free-standing rectangular structure in the ward centre may also be a later feature.

7 km (4.5 miles) NW of Dundalk. NGR: H 996132.

Roodstown Castle

Tower houses became a widespread phenomenon in late medieval Ireland following the collapse of central authority and the resurgence of Gaelic lords. Roodstown is a well preserved, though roofless, example of such a residential tower, with all the typical features – a vaulted ground-floor cellar, a murder-hole inside the main entrance, a well-defended parapet and wall-walk. The windows on the first and second floors have nicely carved 15th-century cusped ogee-headed lights, all with glazing bar holes. The two largest windows, both double lights and one with a transome bar, are in the first-floor hall, which also typically has the

Roodstown Castle

largest fireplace. As is usual in such buildings, the third floor – probably the private chamber – was unheated and had only small rectangular windows.

4 km (2.5 miles) E of Ardee on the Stabannon Road. NGR: N 996925.

County Mayo

Rockfleet Castle

Visitors to this relatively small tower house cannot fail to be delighted by the elegant simplicity of its architecture and by the stark beauty of its setting on an inlet of Crew Bay. But the principal attraction of this romantic place is its association with the legendary Grainne ni Mhaille, Grace O'Malley, who lived here after she married Sir Richard Burke (Richard the Iron) in 1566. Few figures in Irish history catch the imagination more than this remarkable woman, known as the "Pirate Queen", for her undisputed control over the west coast in the late 16th century. Her navy routed large Government seaborne expeditions sent against Rockfleet in 1574 and 1579, while in 1588 she captured ships of the dispersed Spanish Armada and mercilessly killed the crews – an exploit which resulted in her being received in great state by Queen Elizabeth I. After the death of her husband in 1583 she remained at Rockfleet with "all her followers and 1,000 head of cows and mares".

The castle has four storeys with a small rectangular corner turret rising above the parapet. The principal

Rockfleet Castle

apartment must have been in the top floor where there is a fireplace. After the last war the building was restored by the diplomat Sir Owen O'Malley, a direct descendant of Grace, who lived in the nearby late Georgian house. In more recent years it was acquired by a former American ambassador to Ireland.

8 km (5 miles) W of Newport. NGR: L 915954.

County Meath

Athlumney Castle

Tower houses often provided the nucleus for the unfortified country seats that began to emerge in Ireland from the 17th century. Many remain occupied to the present day, but Athlumney, on the east bank of the Boyne, has long been in ruins. It comprises a mid 15th-century tower house, built by the Dowdall family, which was considerably enlarged around 1630 by a long, narrow gabled mansion with large mullioned windows and a fine oriel window. The tower house has four storeys, with an attic and four projecting corner turrets of different sizes containing the stair, latrines and small chambers. In the south wall of the first floor there is a secret mural chamber reached down narrow stairs from above, created – one assumes – to hide priests, for the Dowdalls remained strong Catholics.

The mansion was burnt in 1649 as "one of ye families of ye Maguires was living in it when Oliver Cromwell took Drogheda and to prevent Oliver from getting any shelter or

subsistence there, set ye stately fabric on fire which consumed all ye curious apartments which were said to be very rich and costly".
1.6 km (1 mile) SE of Navan off the Duleek Road. NGR: N 887664.

Donore Castle

The small tower house of Donore may have been built with the premium of £10 that the Government – alarmed by the frequent incursions of Gaelic lords – offered in 1429 to "every liege man" in the Pale who would build "a castle or tower sufficiently embattled or fortified within the next ten years to wit 20 feet in length 16 feet in width and 40 feet in height or more". The inside measurements and height of this simple three-storey rectangular tower certainly meet those requirements. Typically, its lower storeys are vaulted, while it has double-splayed basement loops, a box-machicolation above the ground floor entrance, mural latrine chambers, rounded external corners and a projecting tower at the south-west corner containing the stair.

The little castle came to a very sad end. After it was captured in 1650, the occupants at the time – James, son of MacGeoghegan, and over forty members of his household, including women and children – were all put to death by the Cromwellian general John Reynolds.
13 km (8 miles) SW of Trim on the Kinnegad road, 1 km (0.6 mile) W of Inchamore Bridge. NGR: N 702497.

Trim Castle

Trim Castle is the largest and one of the most important Norman military constructions in Ireland. Its well-deserved reputation as the king of Irish castles rests upon its imposing curtain walls enclosing over three acres, its fine gatehouses and its enormous isolated keep – all of which project a visually striking image of foreboding might and great power.

The first fortification on this site above the banks of the Boyne was a motte erected by Hugh de Lacy in 1172. After this was destroyed by Roderick of Connaught in 1174, de Lacy embarked on building another castle, the nature of which has not yet been established. On the basis of the present limited evidence, it seems likely that the curtain wall and the huge stone keep, which envelopes the stump of the old motte, were begun by de Lacy during the 1170s. Work may still have been proceeding when King John came here in 1210, for the following year, after the Crown had taken control of the castle, the sum of £64 was spent on building work, including "22/- for a large horse … for strengthening the tower". The keep was probably being completed around this time.

The design of the keep is most unusual, comprising a massive square block with towers projecting from the middle of each face (only three out of the original four remain). On plan it looks like a combination of a square and a Greek cross. The towers have thinner walls than the main core and appear to have been added, not for defensive reasons, but to provide extra rooms and possibly because they looked good.

Trim Castle

Three of the four projections have ground floors, but the main core of the keep at this level is evidently filled with earth.

The curtain walls at Trim, two-thirds of which still stand, had a perimeter of 500 yards. They must have been completed by 1224 when William Marshall besieged the castle for seven weeks, for it is unlikely the castle could have withstood his army for such a period without the protection of the curtain walls. There appears to have been a barbican on the town side of the west entrance which was further protected by a murder hole, a portcullis, the gate, and a second murder hole through a hole in the passage. It is often claimed that the upper rooms of this gatehouse were used to house the young Prince Hal, later Henry V, who was left at Trim by Richard II in 1399 before his fateful return to England.

An extensive excavation was carried out in the 1970s in the area between the keep and the south curtain wall. This revealed a stone plinth added to the keep, parts of a ditch possibly dug around the keep and a number of ancillary buildings. It is to be hoped that more excavations will be carried out in the keep itself and in the area near the north tower, where it is evident that the Great Hall of the castle once stood.

Trim. NGR: N 202564.

County Roscommon

Ballintober Castle

This large "keepless" fortress is often claimed to be the only surviving early medieval castle of an Irish ruler. It was built in the 1290s and has a roughly square plan, with enormous asymmetrical polygonal corner towers and a gateway in the eastern curtain, flanked by comparatively small projecting turrets. However, residential apartments in the upper floors of the towers appear quite sophisticated in their design, indicating that Norman rather than Irish architects were employed. Indeed, the oft-repeated claim that this castle was built by the O'Connors of the Royal House of Connaught is difficult to sustain, especially as Irish chiefs of this period had no use for such fortresses. Furthermore, in the 1333 inquisition of the Earldom of Ulster, a hundred court is recorded at Ballintober. It is likely the builder was William de Burgo, and no doubt the castle's large area was intended to permit an Anglo-Norman settlement within its walls. The northern towers are higher than the others as they were rebuilt and repaired in 1627. Outside the walls extra protection was afforded by a wide water-filled moat.

The castle fell into the hands of the O'Connors in the 14th century and remained in their possession for many centuries, being the chief seat of the O'Connor Don from 1385 until 1652. In 1598 it was surrendered to Red Hugh O'Donnell, who attacked it with cannon, breached its walls and forced Hugh O'Connor Don to recant his allegiance to the Crown. In 1641 it became a centre of Catholic resistance with the result that it was confiscated in 1652. The O'Connors regained possession in 1677 and remained in residence until 1701, when it was abandoned.

17.5 km (11 miles) NW of Roscommon off the Tulsk Road.

NGR: M 729748.

Rinnduin Castle

The impressive ruins on the remote Rinnduin Peninsula at Lough Ree have quite a romantic appeal, though they are very overgrown and frustrating to study. The first castle and town was founded here by Geoffrey de Marisco in 1227 as a base during his campaign west of the Shannon. Once the Normans secured a greater foothold in Connaught, Rinnduin assumed an increasingly important position in government military strategy. By the 1270s it was providing a vital link between the royal forts of Roscommon and Athlone, as well as guarding the ships along the Shannon and helping to keep the O'Connor kings of Connaught in check.

The castle is protected by a wide moat, once filled with water, running across the peninsula. This was probably dug in 1227, but the ward wall behind, which has small square loopholes, may not have been completed until 1260. The ward was entered through a rounded-headed archway of cut limestone with slots for a portcullis, outside of which are masonry piers for a bridge that was repaired in 1278.

A town developed under the protection of the castle, defended on the landward side by a substantial towered wall. Only the ruins of the parish church remain, to the east. The town was sacked by the O'Connors in 1236 and 1270. After its final plunder in 1315 it appears not to have recovered. 17.5 km (11 miles) N of Athlone and 4 km (2.5 miles) E of Lecarrow. Access through fields for half a mile to end of peninsula. NGR: N 008539.

Roscommon Castle

Strategically set deep in the plains of Connaught, this great royal fortress was raised as part of a campaign to assert Crown authority west of the Shannon. The first fort was begun in 1269 by Robert de Uffort, but this was demolished by the native Irish under Hugh O'Connor in the 1270s. After this failure, the justiciary embarked on a stronger, more impregnable fortress, built in the early 1280s to the latest military specifications. Similar to Harlech Castle, which it pre-dated by three years, this castle comprised a large quadrangle with projecting D-shaped corner towers and an unusually fine twin-towered gatehouse in the centre of the east wall. A moat with drawbridges surrounded the castle at some distance from the walls, presumably filled from a lake that formerly lay close by.

The castle was stormed in 1308 by a local chief, Donogh O'Kelly, and most of the inhabitants were slain. It remained in Irish hands, though probably largely deserted, until recovered by Sir Henry Sidney from the O'Connors in 1569. Nine years later it was granted to the Governor of Connaught, Sir Nicholas Malby, who built a splendid manor house on the east and north sides of the courtyard, with large mullioned windows inserted into the old walls. This appears to have had gardens on the east side enclosed by high walls with bastions. From 1645 to 1652 the castle was occupied by Confederate Catholics, but was dismantled

Roscommon Castle

after surrendering to the Cromwellians.
Near Roscommon town off the Tulsk road. NGR: M 874649.

County Sligo

Ballinafad Castle

This neat little castle was built as a government military post by Captain St Barbe around 1590 to defend an important pass through the Curlew Mountains, and hence is known as the Castle of the Curlews. It comprises an oblong block of three storeys over a raised basement with stout towers at the corners. There were square rooms in all the towers save the north, where there was a circular timber stair. The door at first-floor level was secured with a drawbar and had an internal grille or gate.

In the early 17th century the castle was garrisoned by a constable and ten warders. In 1642 it was attacked by the insurgent Irish and its defenders were forced to surrender due to lack of water.
Ballinafad village, 9.5 km (6 miles) N of Boyle on the Sligo Road. NGR: G 7808.

Ballymote Castle

Ballymote, begun in 1300, was the last and the mightiest of the Norman castles in Connaught. It was built some distance from an earlier motte by Richard de Burgo, the great Red Earl of Ulster, in order to protect his newly won possessions

Ballinafad Castle

in Sligo. Almost square in plan with massive round towers at each angle, it is the most symmetrical of all the Irish "keepless" castles and bears an unmistakable resemblance to the inner ward of Beaumaris in Anglesea. There was a formidable double-towered gate in the centre of the north wall; recent excavations revealed that the gate towers, now largely demolished, were protected by a double skin of external walling. A postern gate planned for the centre of the south wall was never completed, probably because of the events of 1317, when the castle was lost to the O'Connors.

Possession of the castle from 1317 until 1584 alternated between the O'Connors and the MacDonaghs. A lack of occupation levels implies that the building was virtually abandoned during these years. In 1584 it was taken by the notorious governor of Connaught, Richard Bingham, and remained an English base until lost to Red Hugh O'Donnell in 1598. It was here that O'Donnell assembled his forces on route to Kinsale in 1601. In 1652 the castle was surrendered by the Taaffes to parliamentary forces, and in 1690 it was captured by the Williamites, who soon afterwards had it dismantled and the moat filled in.

Ballymote village, 24 km (15 miles) S of Sligo town. NGR: G 660154.

County Tipperary

Ballynahow Castle

There is something rather attractive about round tower

houses, but sadly only a relatively small number were built, mostly in Munster. Perhaps the finest to survive is the impressive early 16th-century tower of the Purcells at Ballynahow. It stands five storeys high with two internal vaults, each covering two storeys; the top storey was formerly covered by a conical timber roof carried on squinch arches. Both the lower floors were dimly lit round chambers that were probably used for storage, though their size was relatively small because of the wall's thickness at this level. The three storeys above were larger and approximated to a rectangular shape, with ogival and segmental headed windows. One of the thicker segments of the wall was cleverly used to contain the entrance porch with its murder hole, the winding stair, the latrines and a number of other mural chambers. A number of small musket holes can be

Ballymote Castle

found near some of the principal windows.

5 km (3 miles) W of Thurle, off the Ballycahill Road. NGR: S 082602.

Burntcourt Castle

The magnificent shell of this great 17th-century embattled house derives its peculiar name from being burnt by the Parliamentary army on their march to Cahir in 1650. Cromwell himself mentions stopping at the "stronghouse called Clogheen, belonging to Sir Richard Everard", though there is a tradition that Lady Everard set fire to it prior to his arrival. This gave rise to an old rhyme saying, "It was seven years in building, seven years in living and fifteen days in burning." Sir Richard Everard – a distinguished Catholic Royalist and leading member of the Kilkenny Confederation – was hanged by Ireton in 1651, and his castle, quaintly referred to as "Burnt-Clogheen" in an inquisition of 1693, was never rebuilt.

The stronghouse was erected on lands granted to Sir Richard Everard by Charles I in 1639. A datestone recording the building's completion in 1641 was once placed over one of the doors, but now is inserted in the wall at the entrance to the nearby farmyard. That year Sir Richard and his family left their old ancestral castle at Ballyboy to take up residence at their splendid new home. Known at the time as Clogheen, it was one of the largest private dwellings then built in Ireland and comprised a centre block of two storeys over a raised basement with a gabled attic and four gabled corner towers

– the whole building having no less than twenty-six gables. The large number of regularly disposed two-and three-mullioned windows gives the building a quiet, residential air, but its basic design is defensive, notably the use of corner towers, which permits flanking fire along each face of the house. There are pistol loops in the jambs of the back door opening out of the kitchen in the south end, and also in the front entrance on the west side, which has a nicely cut hood moulding with celtic motifs around it, very similar to Monkstown Castle, County Cork.

During the 18th century the artist Anthony Chearnley built a two-storey, five-bay gable-ended house in the bawn and laid out formal gardens outside the bawn wall. A number of engravings, based on drawings by him of Burntcourt, show the ruins as they are now, except that the chimney stacks were then complete.

14 km (8.5 miles) SW of Caher and 6.5 km (4 miles) NE of Ballyporeen. NGR: R 951181.

Cahir Castle

Superbly set on a rocky island in the River Suir, this impressive 15th-century castle – the largest of its period in Ireland – was considered impregnable until the advent of heavy cannon. Described by one Elizabethan commentator as "the bulwark for Munster and a safe retreat for all the agents of Spain and Rome", it fell to Devereux, Earl of Essex, in 1599 after it had been battered for two days with artillery. It surrendered without a fight to Inchiquin in 1647 and again to

Cromwell in 1650, but otherwise had a notably undistinguished history, which possibly helps to explain why it survives in such remarkably good condition today.

Making excellent use of the rocky terrain, its layout comprised a series of courts which cleverly served as successive lines of defence, so that each ward or court dominated the one outside. The core of the castle is surrounded by very thick curtain walls, the lowest parts of which belong to the original fortress on the site built by Philip of Worcester in the 13th century. The massive wall-footing across the middle ward marks the south perimeter of this early castle, while the large adjacent building, known as the keep, originally served as the gatehouse, with a passage through the centre flanked by guard chambers. After this was converted into the main residential block of the castle in the 15th century, the gate was moved alongside, possibly with its original arch. The double machicolation over this entrance is largely an 1840s reconstruction, but the adjacent round tower, which served as a prison, may also have 13th-century foundations.

The present castle appears to be largely the work of Seamus Gallda (James the Foreigner), ancestor of the Butlers, Barons of Cahir. After the death of his father, the third Earl of Ormonde, in 1405, James Butler made Cahir his principal seat and embarked on a building programme. By 1599 the castle had reached its present appearance as illustrated in *Pacata Hibernia*. The only subsequent alterations took place in the 1840s when Richard Butler restored the castle and replaced the picturesque Irish

Cahir Castle

battlements with more solid English ones. The great hall on the east side of the inner ward was also rebuilt at this time though its original form extended much further south; indeed, the main fireplace now lies outside in the open.

The Butlers ceased to occupy the castle in the 18th century and built a house in the town, now the Cahir House Hotel. In the 1860s they erected a mansion, Cahir Park, in the magnificent parkland which adjoins the old castle.
Cahir town. NGR: S 048248.

Carrick-on-Suir Castle

This castle of the Butlers – Earls and later Dukes of Ormonde – stands above the Suir and was acquired in 1515, though the oldest part of the castle is a mid 15th-century walled bawn with a tower house in each of its northern corners. Sometime after 1565 the tenth, or "Black", Earl of Ormonde, who spent many years in the court of his cousin Queen Elizabeth I, added a Tudor manor house of a type common in England but like no other in Ireland. The low U-shaped range of this house forms three sides of a small court attached to the old bawn, whose towers rise behind it. It has two storeys with a gabled attic, rows of mullioned windows and steep brick gables with slender finials. There are few defensive features save for small firing holes either side of the front door.

The house was a favourite haunt of the Great Duke of Ormonde, but afterwards it was deserted by the family although they continued to own it until the present century.

Fortunately, it was never allowed to fall into complete ruin and in 1947 was taken over by the State, who subsequently conserved the building. Their most notable achievement was the restoration of the long gallery on the first floor of the front elevation, whose ceiling had largely collapsed. This delightful room, once hung with tapestries, has a magnificent limestone mantel bearing the date 1565, and stucco representations of Queen Elizabeth I flanked by Equity and Justice. The Queen would have felt at home in this room and in the rest of this house, which was probably intended, for she is believed to have promised her favourite cousin "Black Tom" that she would one day honour Carrick with a visit. Carrick-on-Suir. NGR: S 405216.

Nenagh Castle

The finest cylindrical keep in Ireland – known to generations of Tipperary people as the "Nenagh Round" – was built around 1200 by Theobald Walter, the founder of the great Butler dynasty of Ormonde. It formed the north corner of a pentagonal court with a towered gatehouse on the southern side and strong towers on the north-west and south-east angles. This has now vanished, save for fragments of the gatehouse and east tower, but the keep survives to a height of 100 feet. Its topmost quarter was added about 1860 by the Bishop of Killaloe in emulation of Windsor Castle – the original height to the wall-walk being about 75 feet.

There were four storeys, including a basement, with a first-floor entrance giving access to a winding mural stair that was once enclosed by a protecting turret. The second and third floors have narrow loops with large embrasures for crossbowmen, but the top floor is well lit by four windows and was clearly the main chamber.

The Butlers remained at Nenagh until the 14th century, when they moved to Gowran and later purchased Kilkenny Castle in 1391. During the 15th century it was occupied by the O'Briens, but was recovered in 1533 by Sir Piers Ruadh Butler, later Earl of Ormonde. The castle changed hands many times before and during the Cromwellian wars, but after its capture by Ginkel in 1690, the place was dismantled by the Williamites. The Butler link was finally broken in 1703 when the second Duke of Ormonde sold the place to pay debts.

Nenagh. NGR: R 865764.

County Tyrone

Benburb Castle

The name Benburb, roughly translated as "proud peak", aptly describes the setting of this Plantation bawn, perched on the summit of a limestone cliff towering 200 feet above the River Blackwater. It was built in 1611–14 by Sir Richard Wingfield (later Viscount Powerscourt) who was granted 1,000 acres here from James I. An earlier castle on or close to the site was the "chief seat" of the celebrated Shane O'Neill, before it was burnt in 1566.

Benburb Castle

The bawn occupies a large irregular quadrangular area enclosed by walls standing almost to full height and generously fitted with musketry loop-holes. No main house was built as Wingfield had no desire to live here, but living accommodation was provided in gabled rectangular flankers incorporated into corners of the bawn. One of these was occupied in 1622 by "Mr Moore, an Englishman, with his wife and family". In the south-east corner of the enclosure is a round stair turret giving access to a postern down the cliff, while the house on the south-west side was built in the late 18th century and remodelled in Victorian times.

The castle was captured in 1641 by Phelim O'Neill, who had all the inmates put to death. In 1646 it was occupied by Owen Roe O'Neill before he defeated the English army at the battle of Benburb. It was dismantled soon afterwards and has remained a ruin ever since.

Benburb town. NGR: H 814520.

Castle Caulfield

Sir Toby Caulfield, later Lord Charlemont, must have had a very strong desire to live like an English gentleman, for he was prepared to build an unfortified English-style mansion in an unsettled area of Ulster during the period 1611–19. Described by Pynnar in 1619 as "the fairest building in the north", it had three storeys in a U-shaped plan – the north-west wing of which has now disappeared. It had fireplaces in projecting breasts and massive chimney stacks capped with octagonal stone shafts, as well as flat-headed mullioned and transomed windows, most of which have been torn out. The gatehouse, with its vaulted passage and guard chambers, probably belong to an earlier O'Donnelly bawn on the site.

During the 1641 Rebellion the house was burnt by Patrick "the Gloomy" O'Donnelly and some of the interior stonework still shows signs of scorching. In the 1660s the house was partially rehabilitated by the Caulfields, who were in residence in 1670 when Archbishop Oliver Plunket was permitted to use the courtyard for ordinations. It was probably disused by 1700 and was a ruin when John Wesley preached in front of the gates in 1767.
Castlecaulfield village. NGR: H 755626.

Harry Avery's Castle

A curiously enigmatic castle named after and possibly built by Henry Aimbreidh O'Neill, a Gaelic chief celebrated by the Four Masters for his justice, nobility and hospitality who died

Castle Caulfield

in 1392. The castle commands wide views over the Mourne Valley and is unusual in being a stone-built stronghold located deep in the heart of pre-Plantation Ulster. It consists of a two-storey rectangular block fronted by a pair of massive D-shaped towers – resembling a gatehouse – projecting from the south face of an artificially scarped knoll, whose sides have been revetted by a wall to form a polygonal enclosure, now ruined to a low level with traces of a latrine tower on the north side. Excavations in 1950 and 1962 confirmed that the keep-like structure functioned more as a tower house than as a true gatehouse, though the only access into the enclosure behind seems to have been up a

Harry Avery's Castle

narrow mural stair and through the hall at first-floor level. Other features include vaults with traces of wickercentring and latrine shafts in one of the towers.

The castle was captured by the English in 1609. Subsequently, it was used as a quarry for building material. 1 km (0.6 mile) SW of Newtownstewart, 16 km (10 miles) SE of Strabane. NGR: H 323852.

County Westmeath

Athlone Castle

Athlone used to be one of the most formidable medieval fortresses in Ireland, but warfare and substantial rebuilding have left little of the old castle above internal ground level.

The construction of both a bridge and castle at this key river crossing began in 1210, following King John's visit to Ireland, when Bishop Henry de Grey was ordered to begin settling the middle Shannon region between Meath and Connaught. De Grey's stone tower, probably built on an earlier motte of 1199, had to be rebuilt the following year after it collapsed, killing nine of the garrison. It was again repaired in 1251 and in 1273-9 the curtain walls were probably added, flanked by massive D-shaped towers. Most of this structure was still present when drawn by Thomas Phillips in 1685, together with a fine suite of apartments, used by the Lord President of Connaught, overlooking the river.

The castle's strategic position meant that it saw a good deal of military action. In 1691 it suffered the heaviest

bombardment in Irish history: Williamite General Ginkel attacked with over 600 bombs, 12,000 cannon balls and huge quantities of stones. The whole castle was rebuilt from 1793 to 1815, reduced in height and strengthened for the mounting of heavy cannon in efforts to fortify the Shannon against French invasion. The lower storey of de Grey's polygonal tower is the only part of the medieval fabric to survive.
Athlone town. NGR: N 038413.

County Wexford

Enniscorthy Castle

The town of Enniscorthy developed around this much rebuilt and restored 13th-century castle standing on a rock at the head of the Slaney's navigable tideway.

The original building was probably built by Gerald de Prendergast during the 1230s, and like both Ferns and Carlow, comprised a rectangular keep of four storeys strengthened at the corners by communicating three-quarter drum towers. In 1253 it passed through marriage to the Rochford family, and by the 15th century was held by the MacMurrough Kavanaghs. By the 1530s the castle was evidently in Crown possession and serving as the Seneschal's residence. It was leased to Edmund Spenser for three days in 1581 and five years later was acquired by Sir Henry Wallop. It was captured by Cromwellian troops in 1649 and was used as a prison during the 1798 Rebellion.

During the early 19th century the castle suffered a

restoration by the Earl of Plymouth, and yet another at the end of the century by a local MP who enlarged it and used it as a residence. The building now houses the county museum.

Wexford town. NGR: S 971399.

Ferns Castle

The much-ruined castle at Ferns is the largest of a distinctive group of 13th-century Hiberno-Norman keeps that comprise rectangular blocks with cylindrical corner towers. Known as "towered" or "four-towered" keeps, they evolved independently in the South Leinster region at least a century before any comparable castles were built in England. Considering the great size of the Ferns keep it is perhaps surprising that we have no historical reference for the date of its building, but it was probably begun around 1222 by Earl William Marshall the younger. Architectural details, however, suggest that it was not completed until the mid 13th century, when it was held by William de Valance.

In its heyday the castle must have been particularly imposing. The three storeys of the main block were divided into vast apartments, the upper floors of which were lit by rather splendid trefoil-pointed windows, mostly grouped in pairs beneath pointed and camber-headed embrasures. There are similar windows in the beautiful circular chapel on the second floor of the largely complete south-east tower. This room, often cited as the most perfect chapel to be found in any Irish castle, is particularly noteworthy for its moulded rib-vaulting and supporting corbels in the shape of capitals. Of the other corner towers, one has vanished, only fragments remain of another, while about half survives of the south-west tower, which has a cellar hollowed out of solid rock, said to have been used to keep Kathleen, daughter of William Marshall, to prevent her eloping. Outside the walls a ditch was partly exposed during archaeological excavations carried out in the 1970s.

The castle evidently ceased being a residence in the early 14th century, for the ditch appears to have been filled by about 1310, while the building was in a bad state of repair by 1324. It was captured by the O'Tooles in 1331, recovered by Bishop Charnell shortly afterwards, and seems to have stayed in the hands of the Bishopric of Ferns until the 1370s when it was taken by the MacMurroughs. Lord Grey captured the place during the 1536 revolt, but the MacMurroughs managed to remain until 1551, when it was taken over for the Crown by John Travers. The Mastersons held the castle from 1583 until 1649, when it was surrendered to Cromwellian soldiers. It is likely these troops were responsible for demolishing much of its structure.
Ferns village. NGR: T 017501.

Rathmacknee Castle

Many Irish castles have lost their parapets during the course of time, but those at Rathmacknee are fully intact and are a superb example of the picturesque multi-stepped crenellations so characteristic of late medieval Irish architecture. Other features of the castle have survived equally well, and although now lacking its roof and floors, it may be considered one of the most complete examples of a tower house in South Leinster.

The tower occupies a corner of a well-preserved five-sided bawn that has a boldly projecting machicolation above the entrance. In plan the tower is a simple rectangle with one small projection – a prolongation in the east wall to accommodate latrines. There is a mural stair linking all five storeys, each having one apartment with closets or chambers in the thickness of the wall. The two lower storeys are beneath vaulting, while the timber floors had cross-beams that were tenoned directly into the wall-beams rather than laid directly upon them – an unusual practice that allowed the depth of the floor to be reduced.

It is probable that the castle was built by John Rossiter, Seneschal of the Liberties of Wexford, in 1451, whose family had lived in this area since the 12th century. Though staunch Catholics, they survived the Reformation purges, but ultimately forfeited their lands in the 1650s. The castle remained occupied until the 1760s.

12 km (7.5 miles) SW of Wexford town, off a minor road W of the main Kilmore Road. NGR: T 037143.

Slade Castle

The picturesque little harbour of Slade is dominated by the brown rubble walls and striking merlons of this castle, formerly home of the Laffans, possibly merchants here in late medieval times. The building comprises a tower house built in the late 15th or early 16th century, and an attached two-storey hall of slightly later date.

The tower, standing 56 feet high and gracefully tapered, contains a mural stair in the south-east angle and barrel vaults over the second and fifth floors; above the latter rises a turret accommodating the stair head, a small apartment and the base of what was once a tall chimney stack. The rooms were all very small, including the main chamber on the third floor, which had a latrine, fireplace, cupboard recess and two windows. No doubt the two-storey house was later added to provide more living space. It has its own entrance on the south side, leading via a lobby up a straight mural staircase to three fair-sized rooms on the first floor. A low-pitched slated roof once covered these rooms rising from the wall-walk behind the attractive many-stepped battlemented parapet, though on the east side the roof was at a higher level to accommodate an extra storey. The three ground-floor rooms strangely cannot be entered from the living quarters above and may have been intended as a warehouse on the quay.

The castle was forfeited by the Laffan family in the aftermath of the 1641 Rebellion, though the Laffan heir was only a young boy who could not possibly have been implicated in the war. The building appears to have been used and extended in the late 18th century as part of an extensive salt works adjoining the site.

Located at the E end of Hook Head, 9.5 km (6 miles) SW of Fethard-on-Sea. NGR: X 747986.

Acknowledgements

The publisher would like to thank the following for permission to reproduce work in copyright:

© istockphoto.com/Thomas Johnston (p 34)
© istockphoto.com/John Hornsby (p 18)
© istockphoto.com/Ronn Kilby (p 109)
© istockphoto.com/Marco Radtke (p 42)
© istockphoto.com/Brian Kelly (p 74)
© istockphoto.com/Simon Jeacle (p 96)
© Yoshiko Tabata (p 26)
© Pam McCreight (p 24)

Index to Castles